Mandala Coloring Books Arts: Adults relaxation Meditation, and Happiness. (Volume 1)

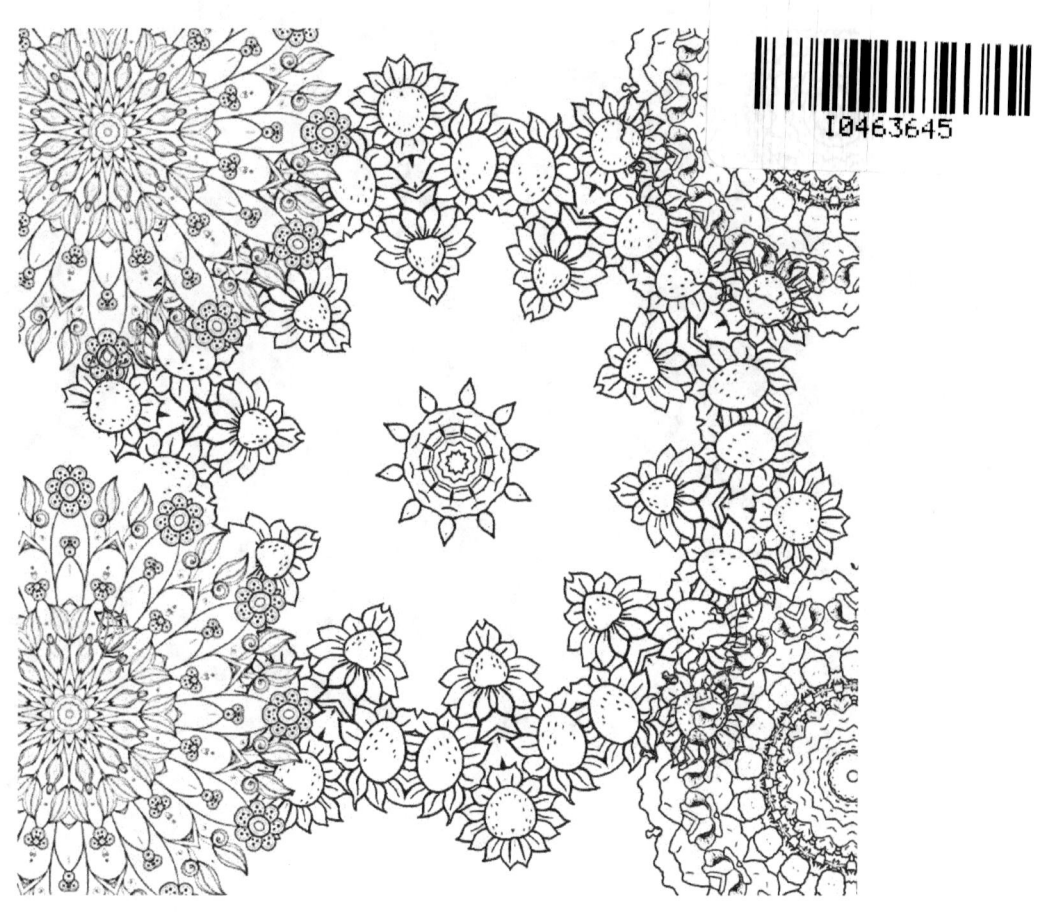

Rosalinda Bradner

Mandala Coloring Books Arts: Adults relaxation Meditation, and Happiness. (Volume 1)

ISBN-13: 978-1543168211

ISBN-10: 1543168213

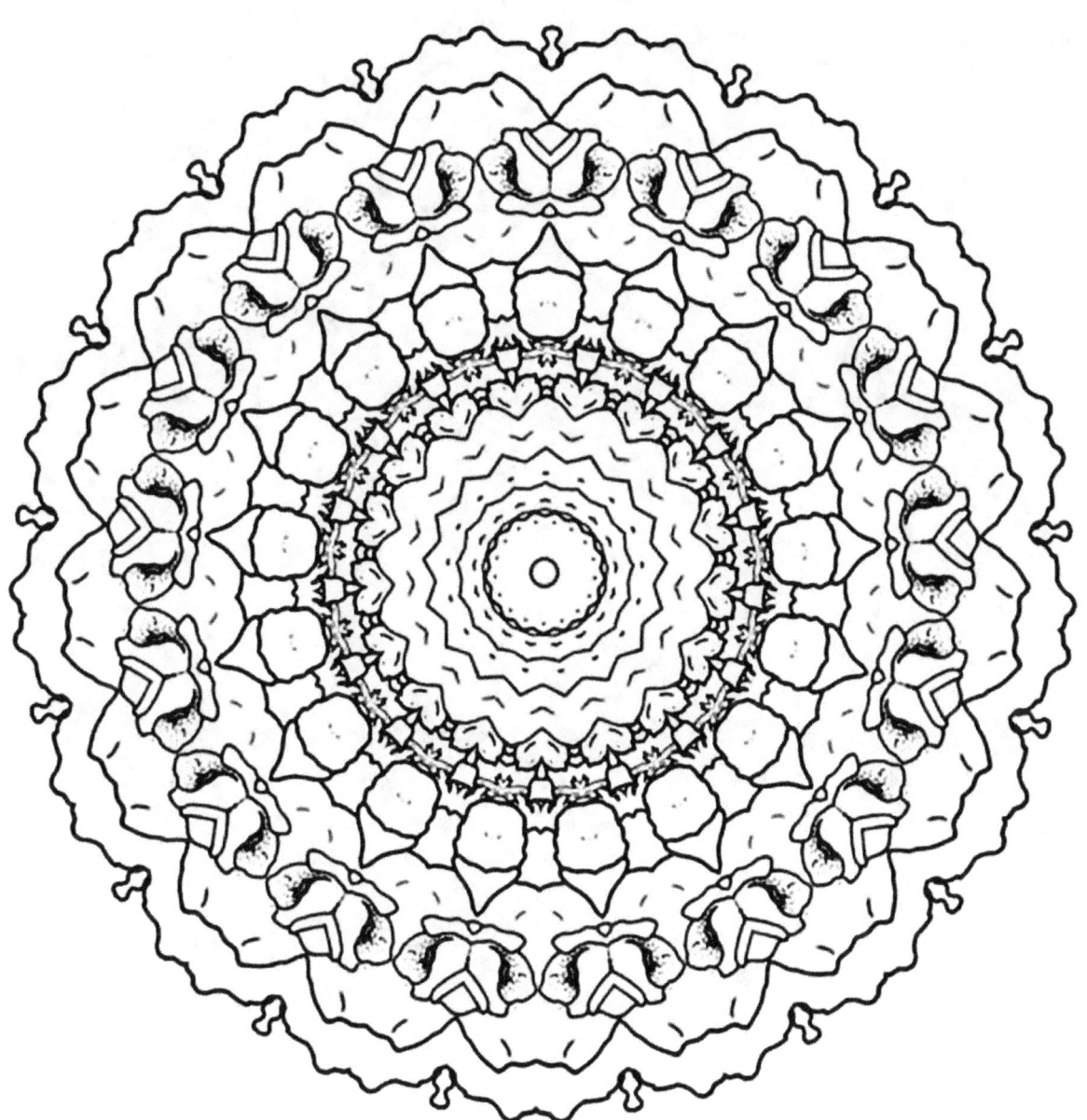

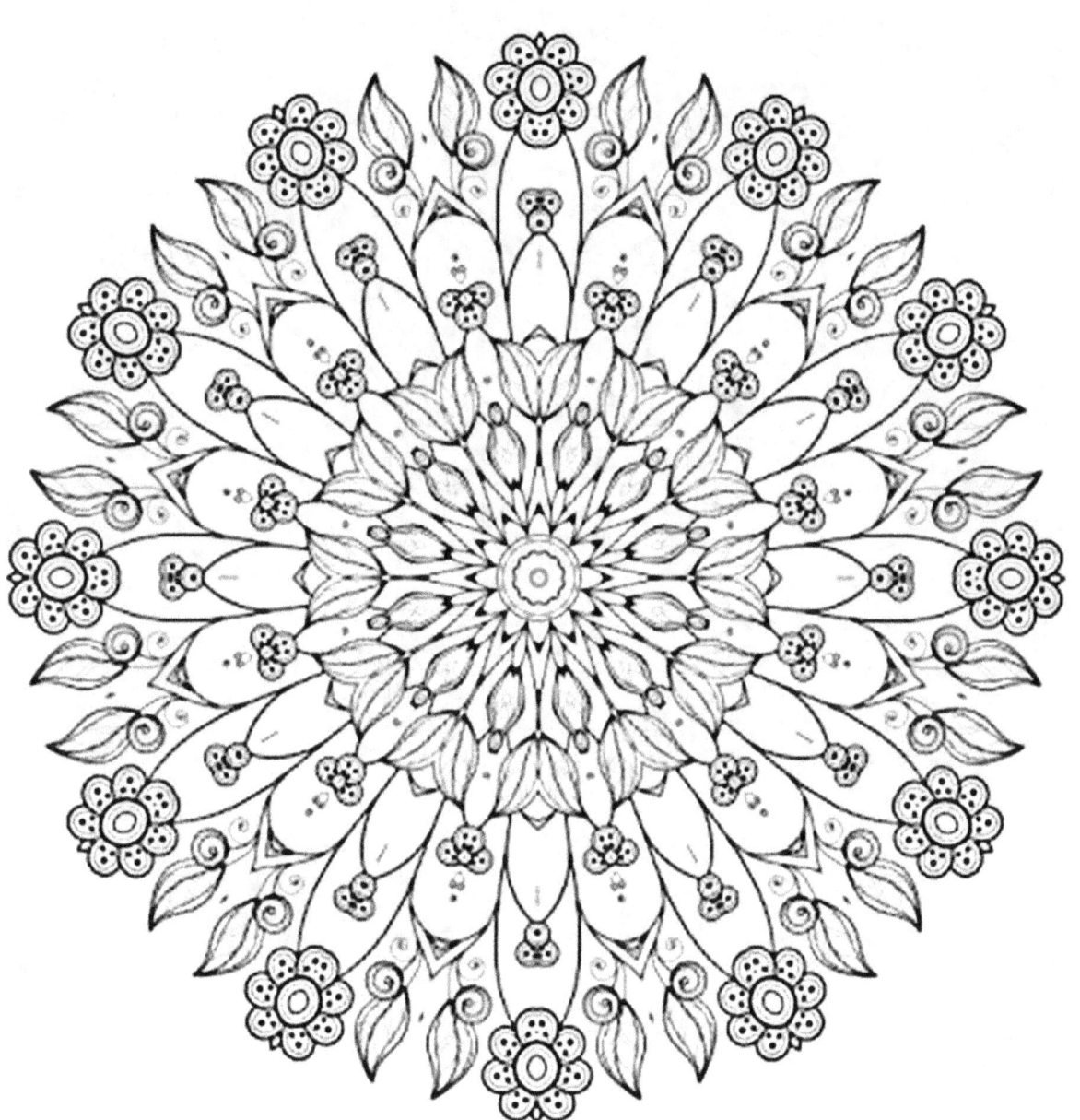

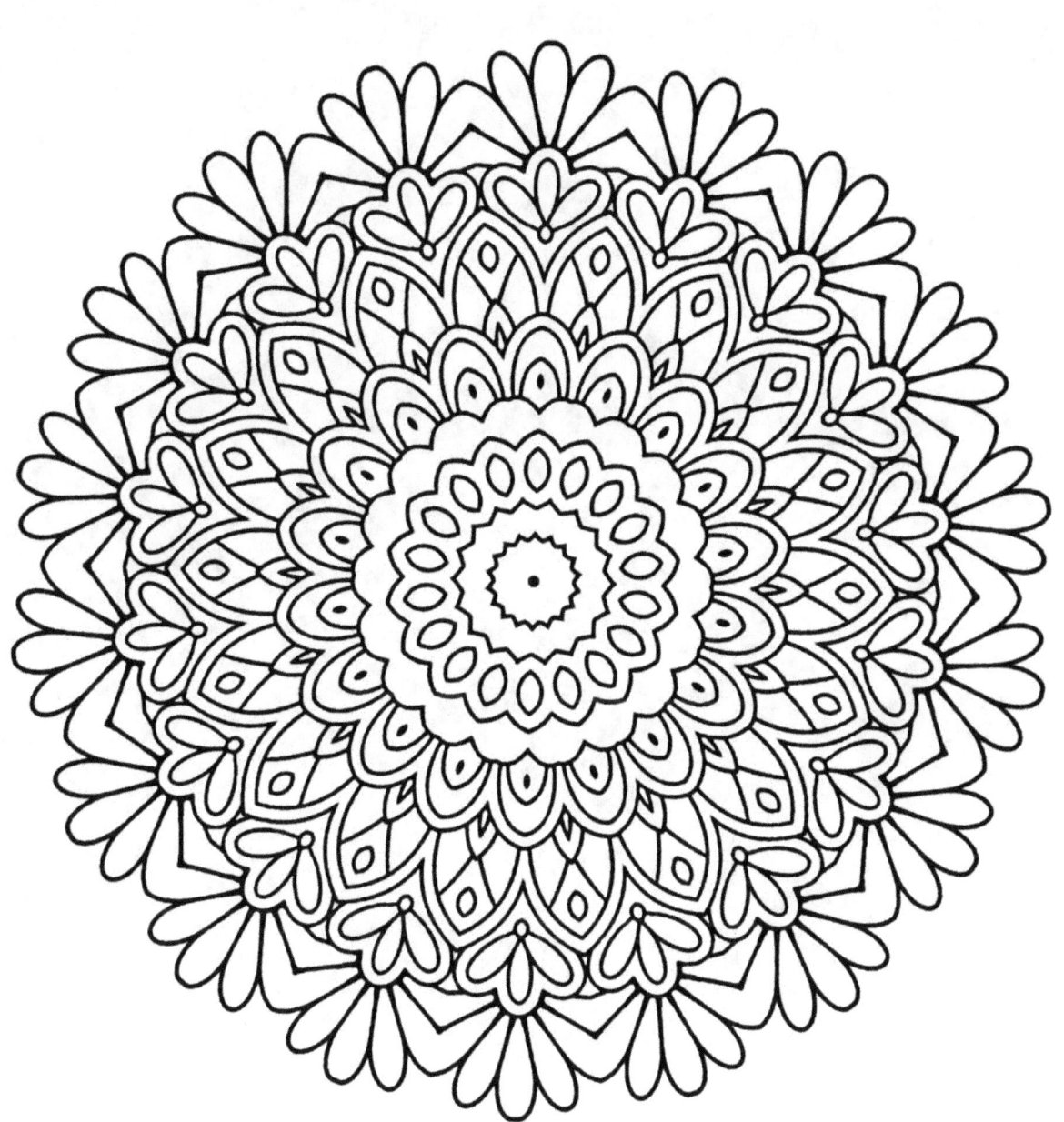

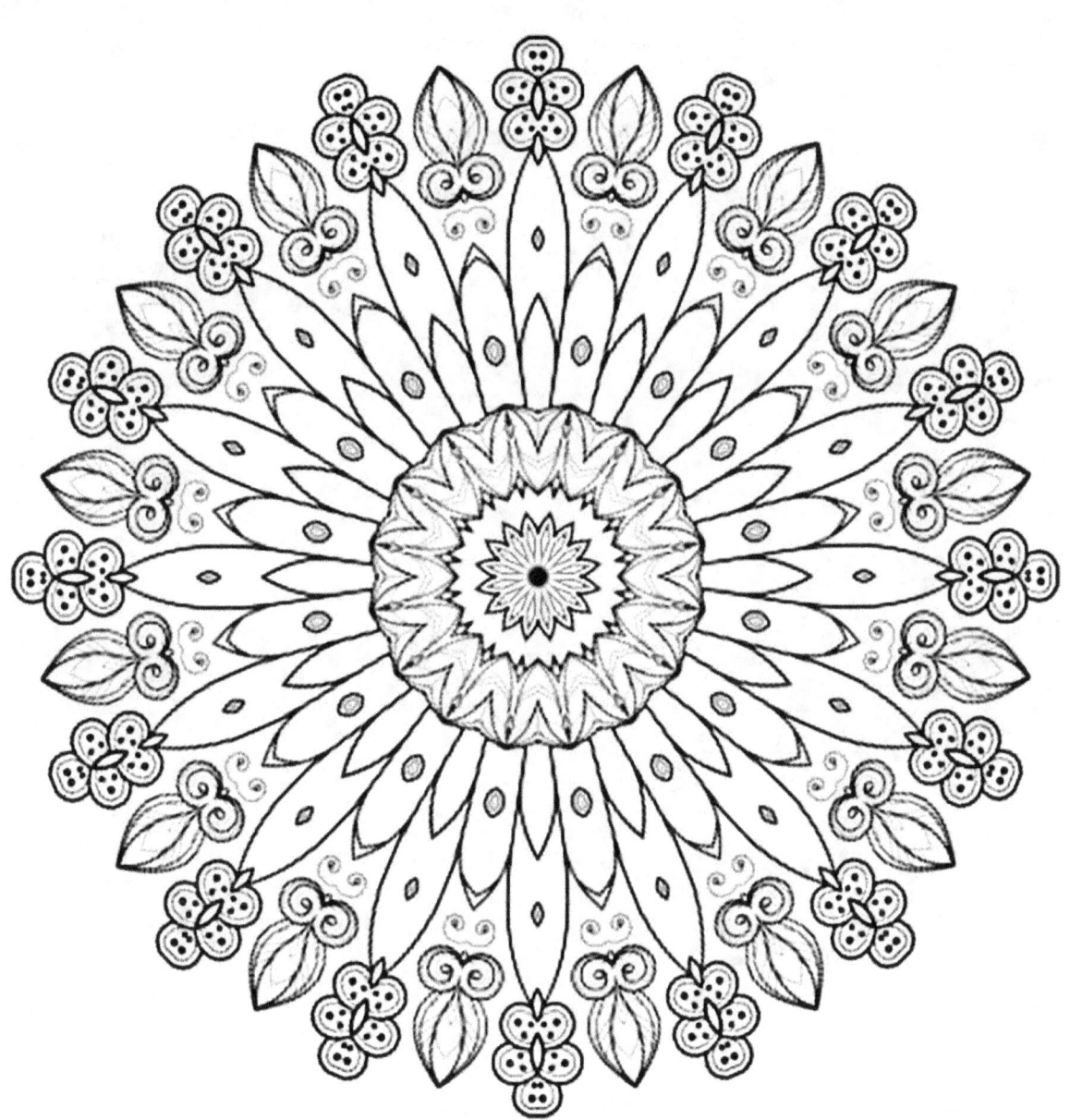

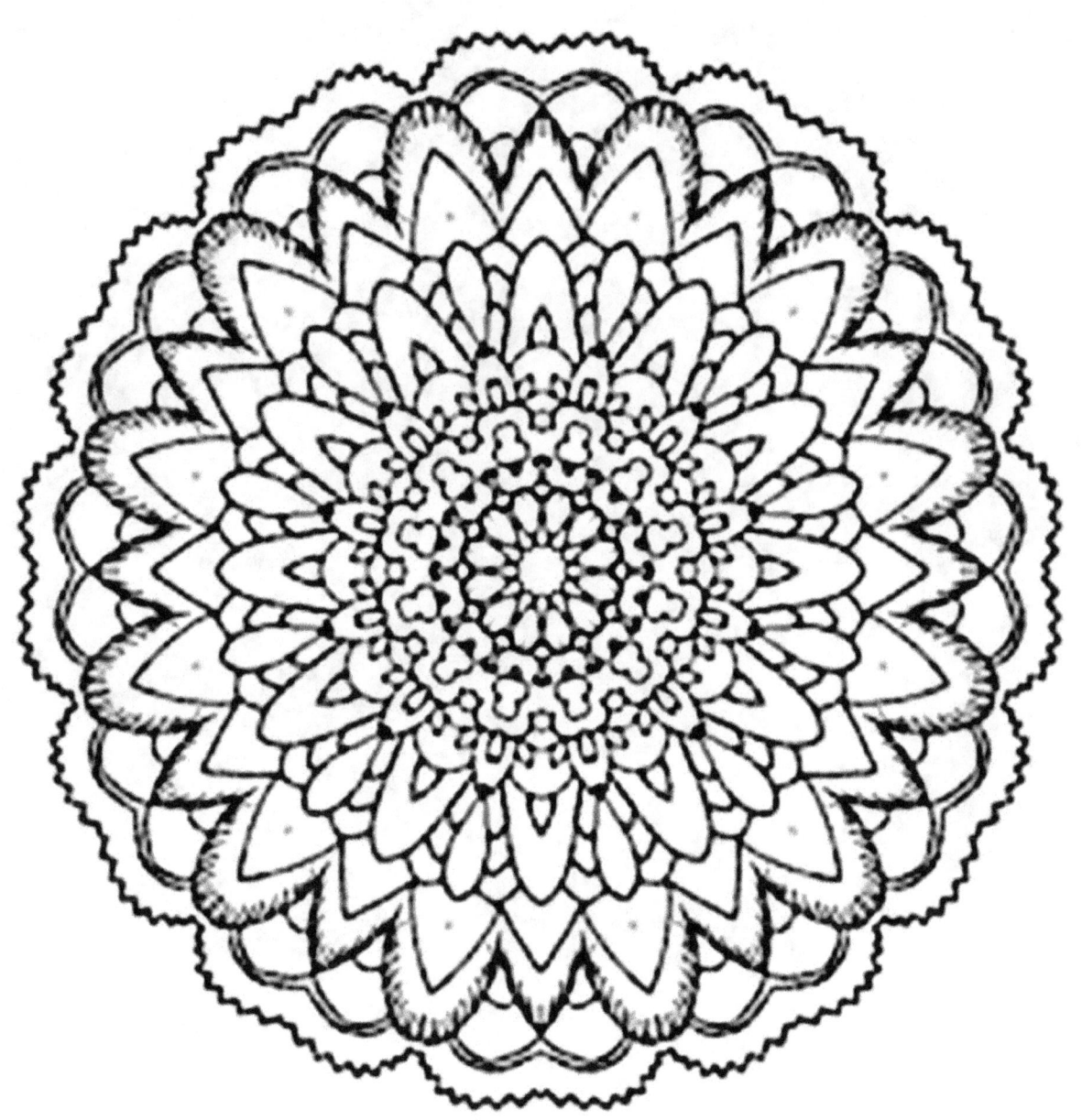

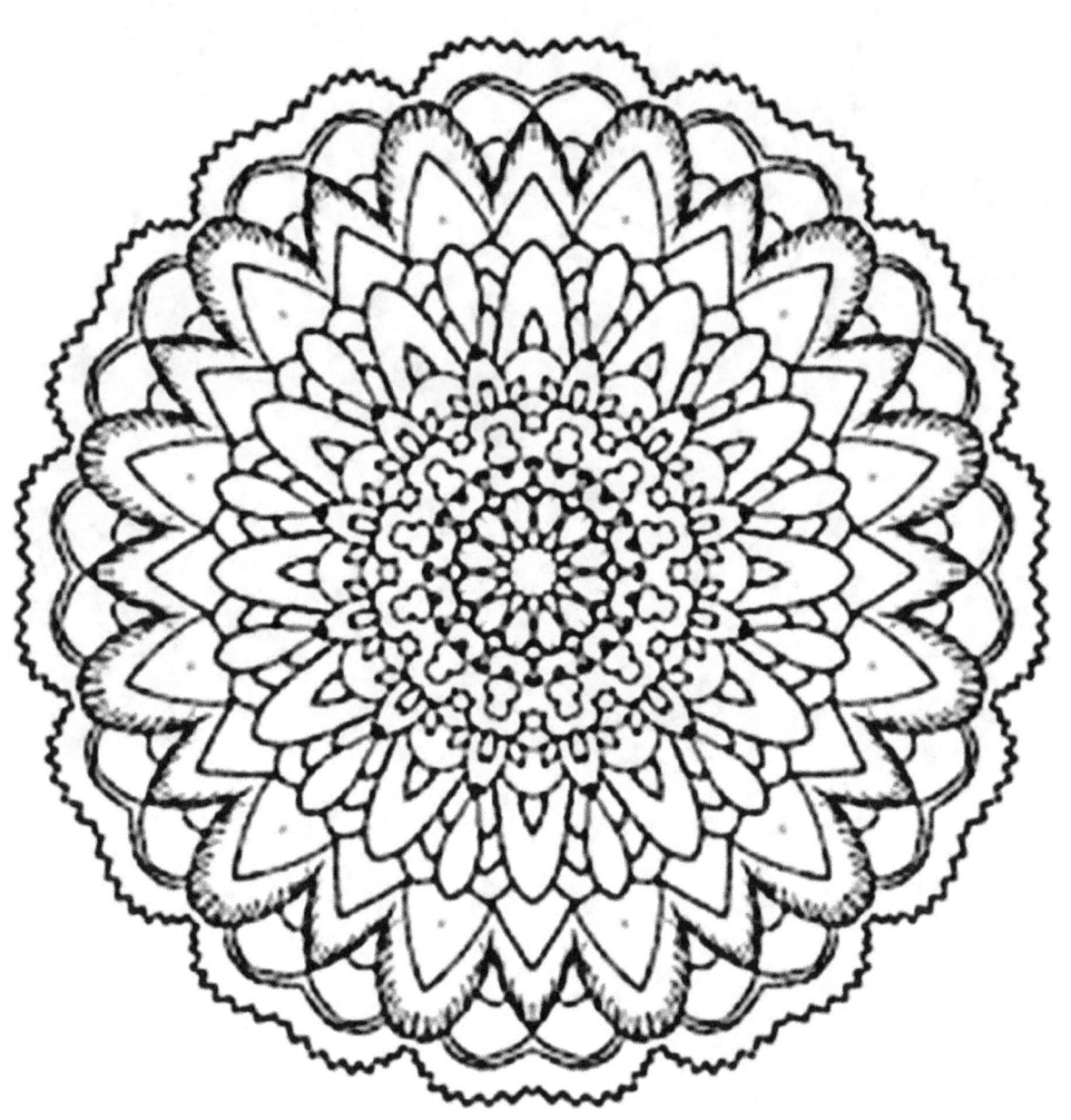

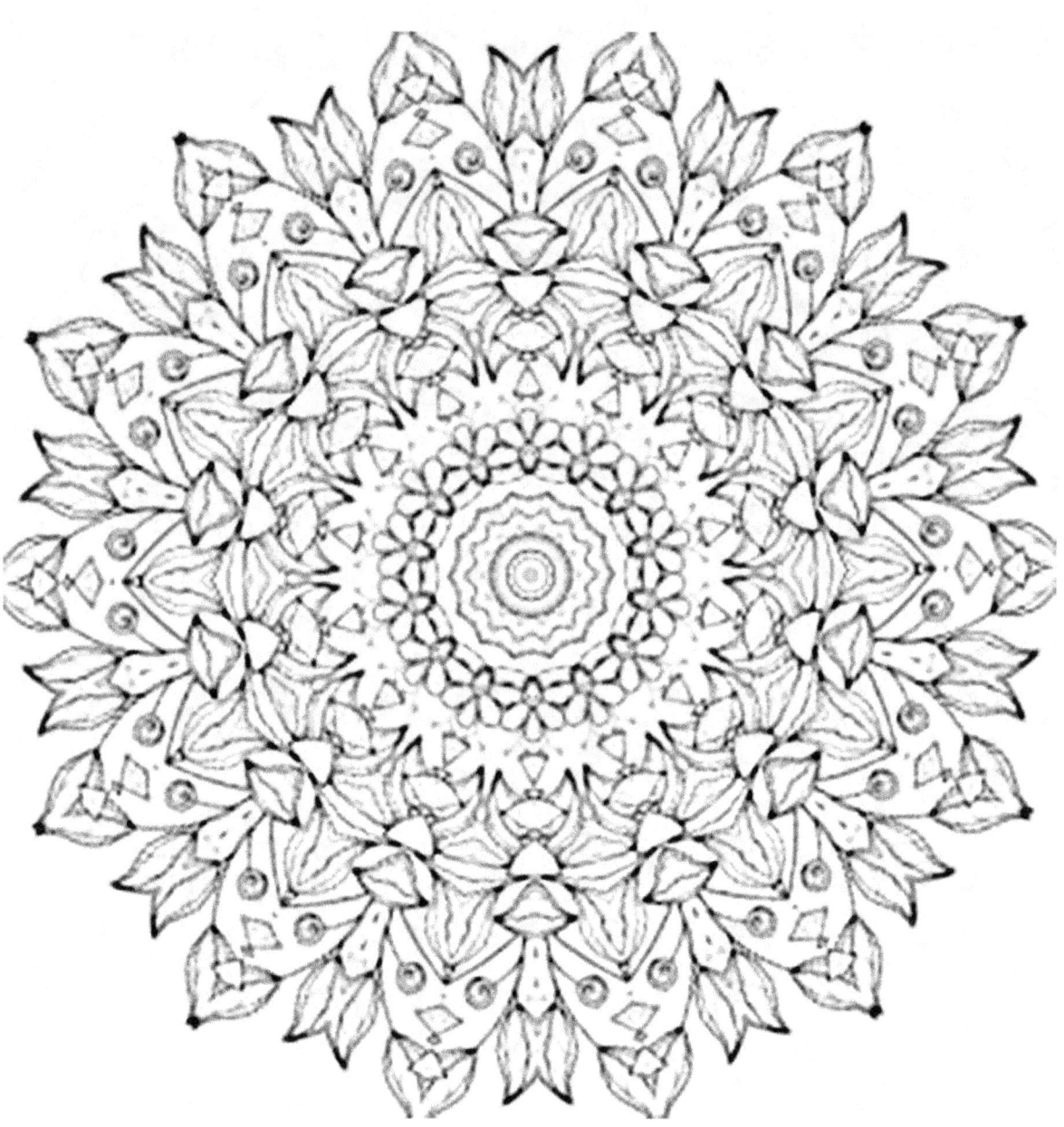

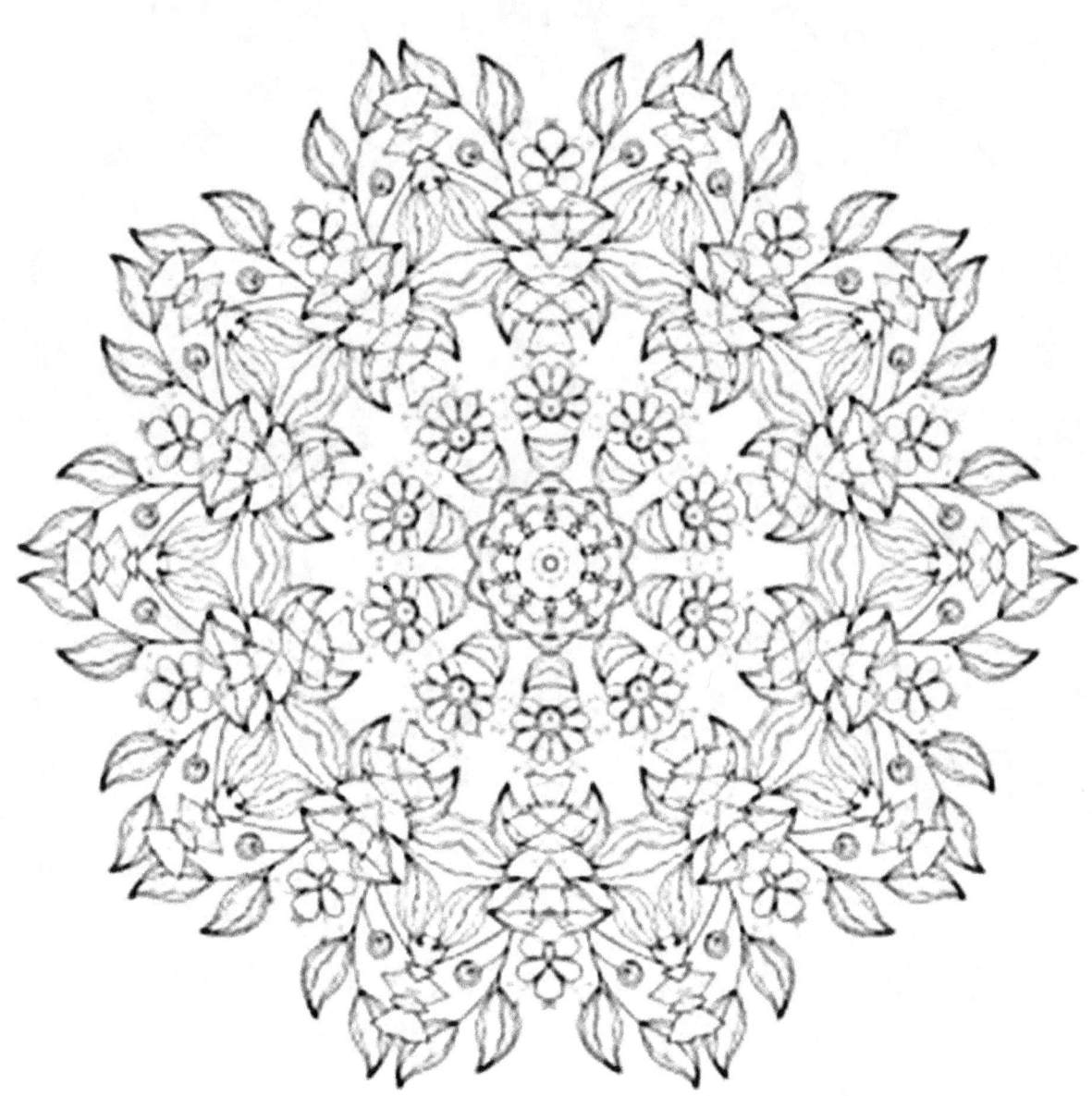

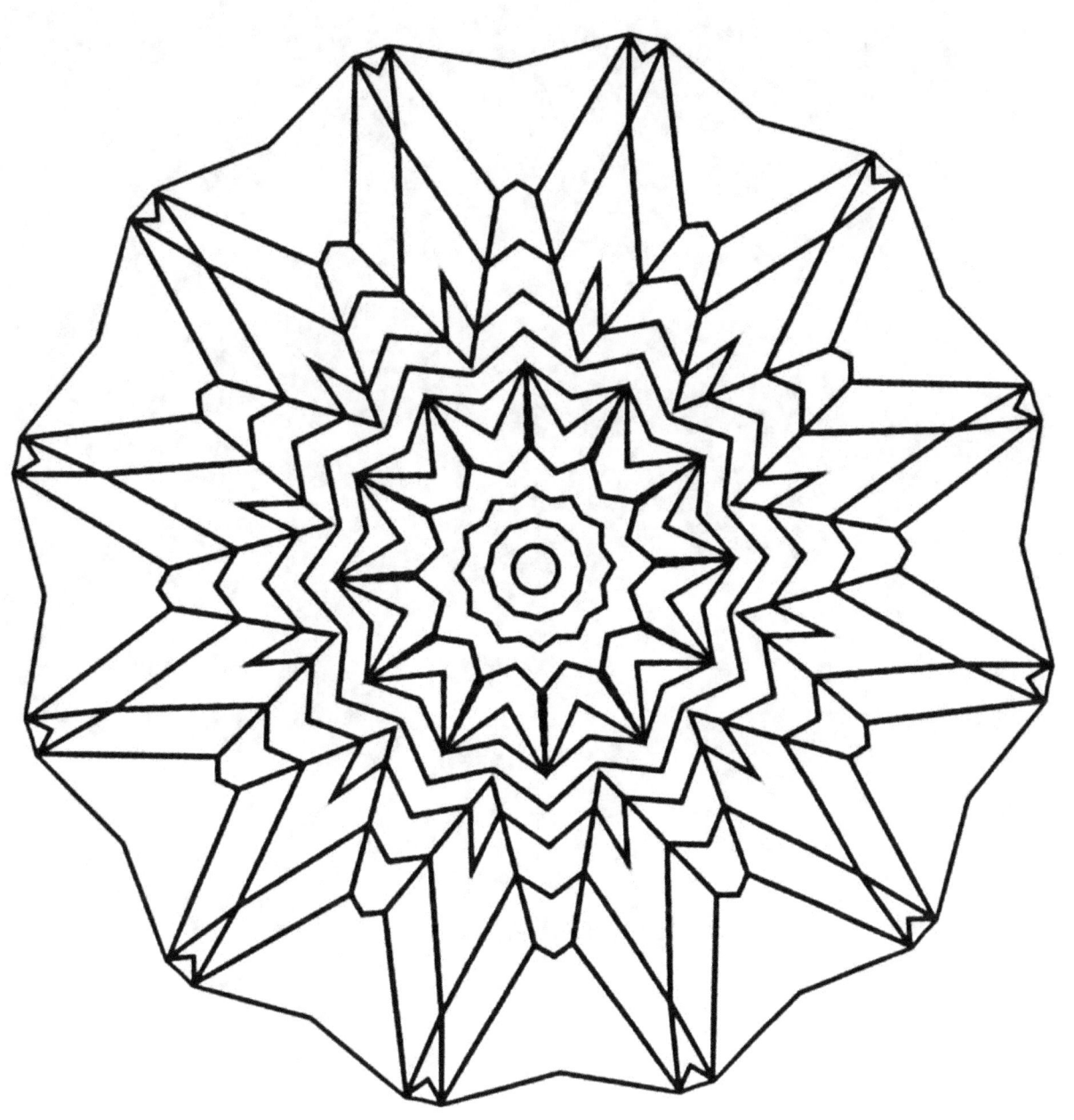

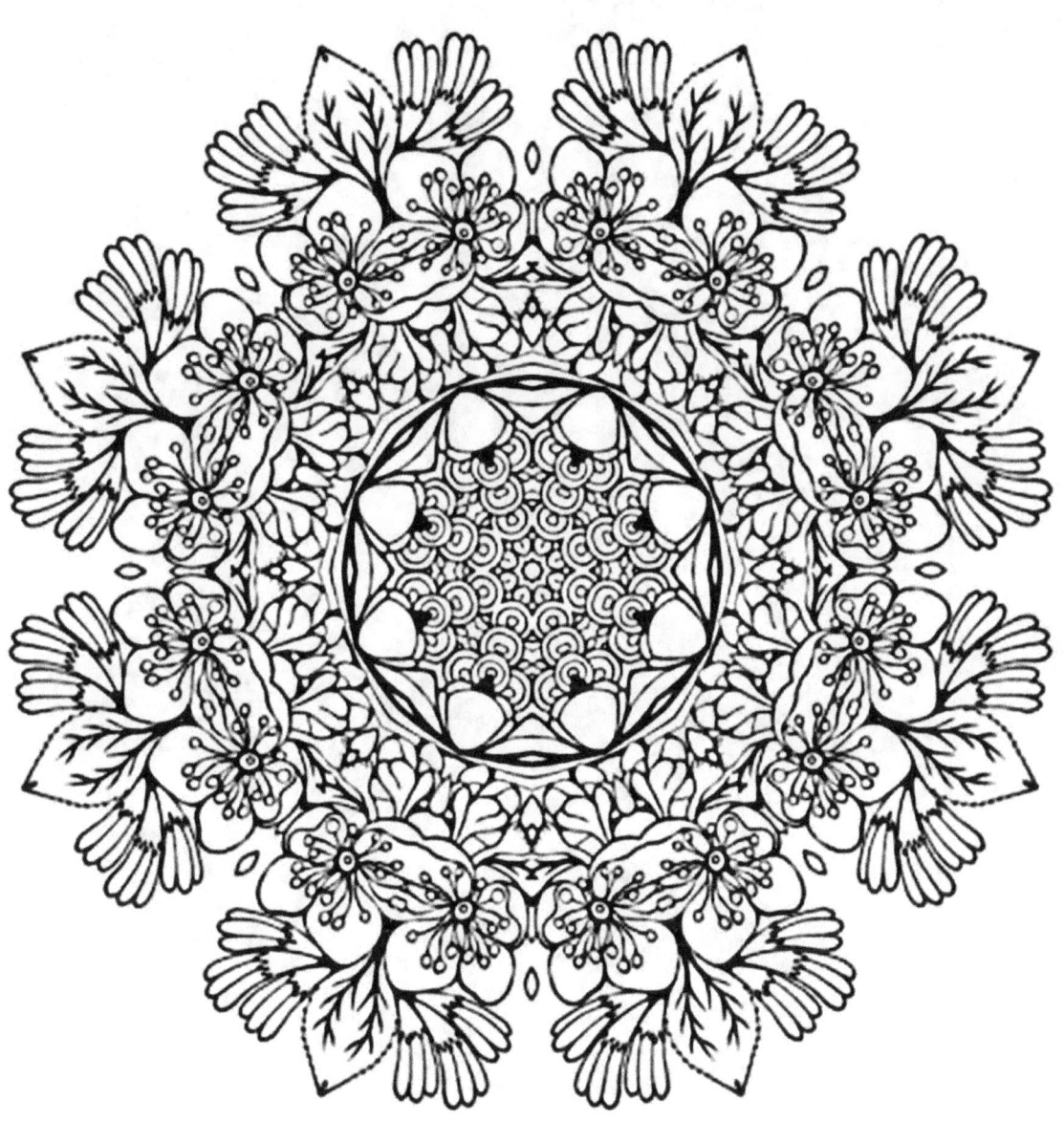

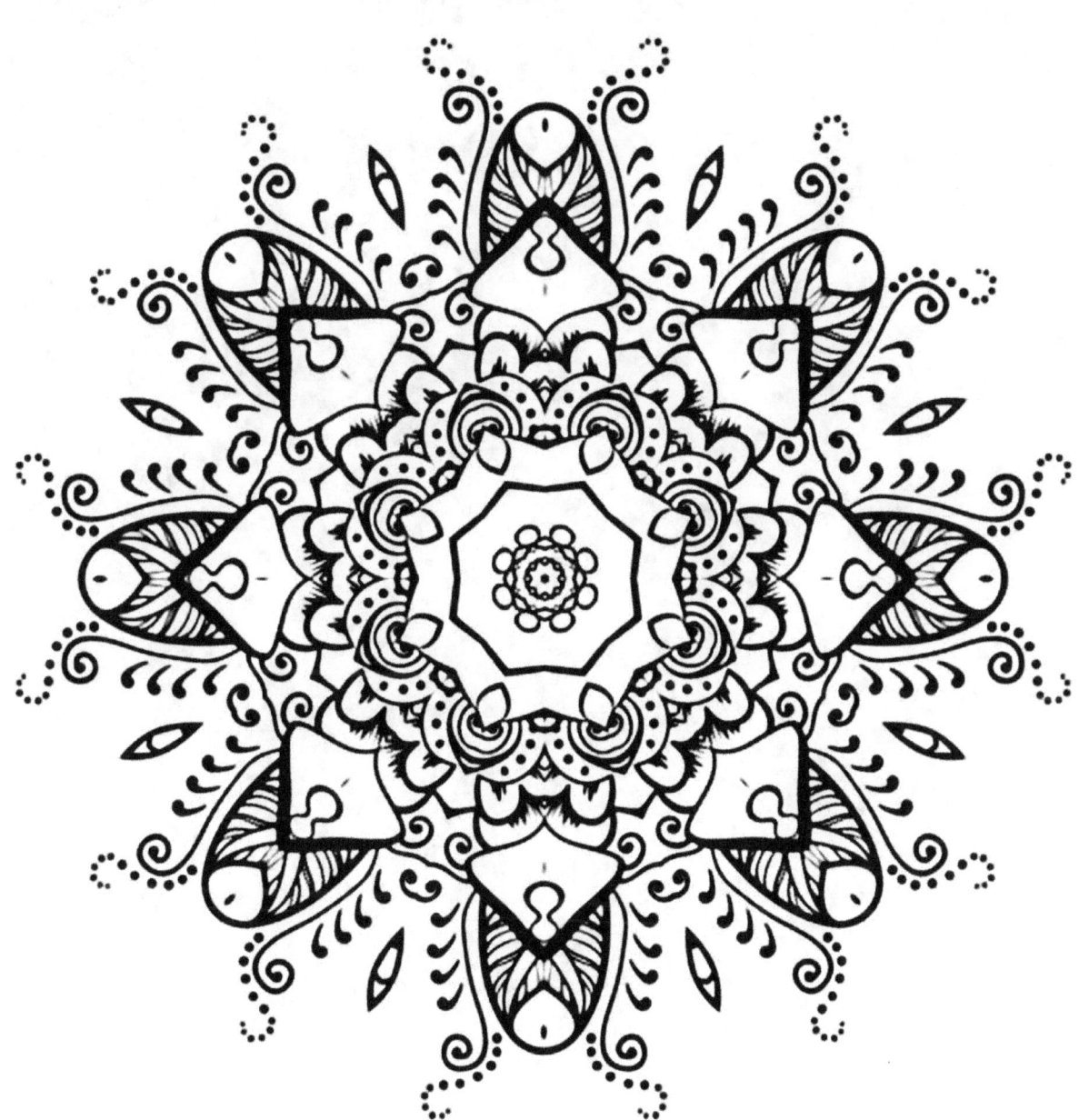

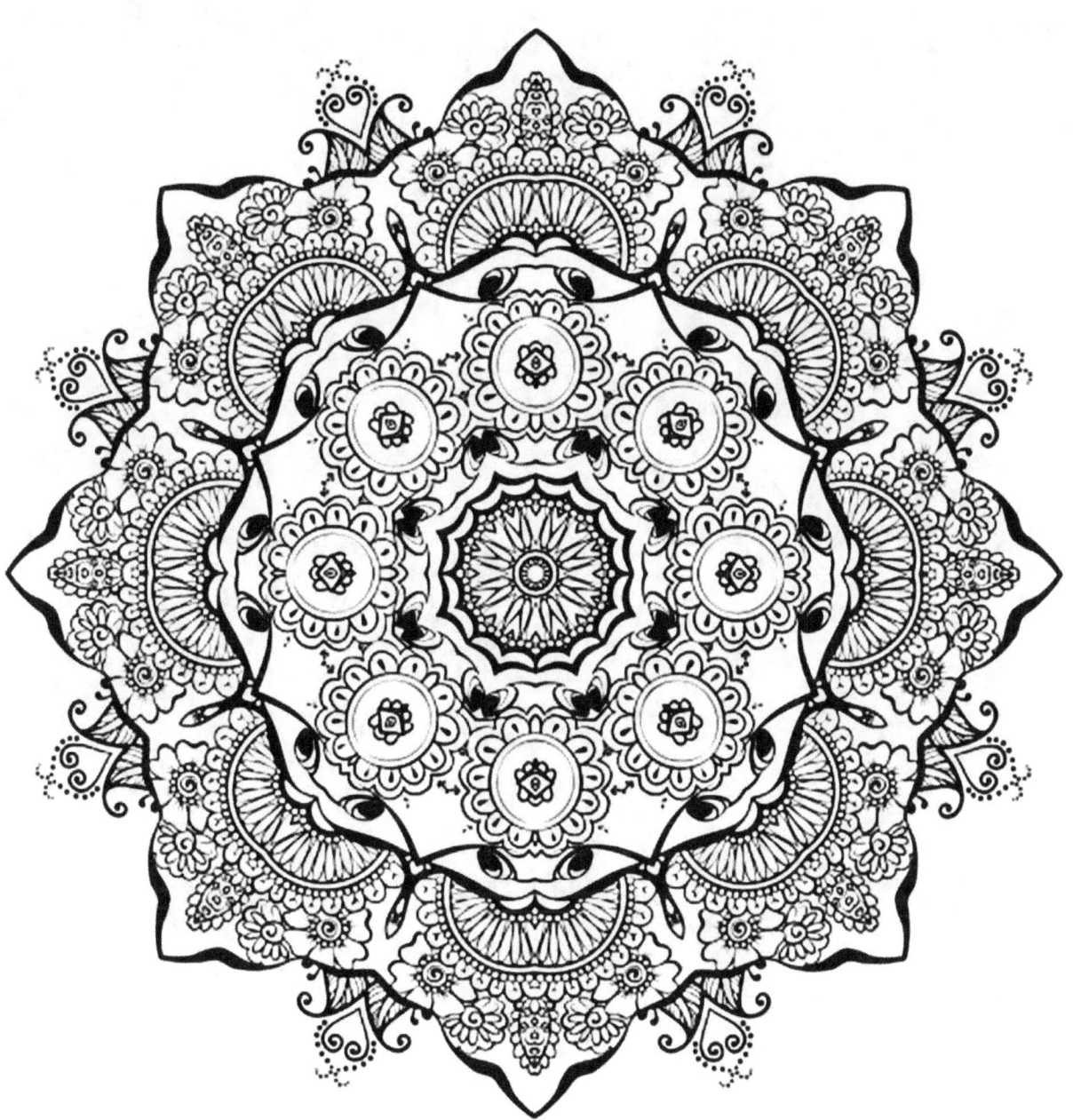

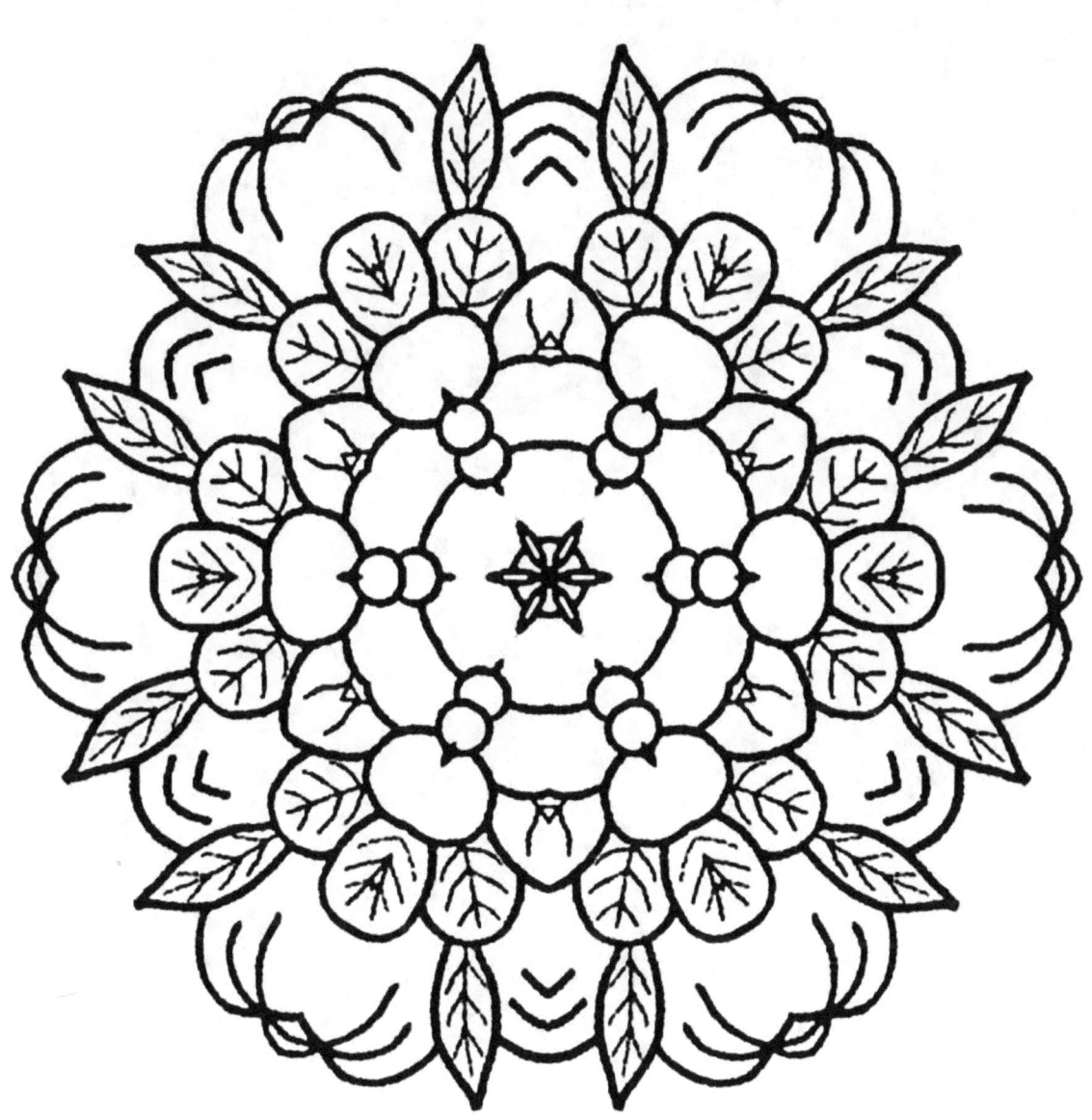

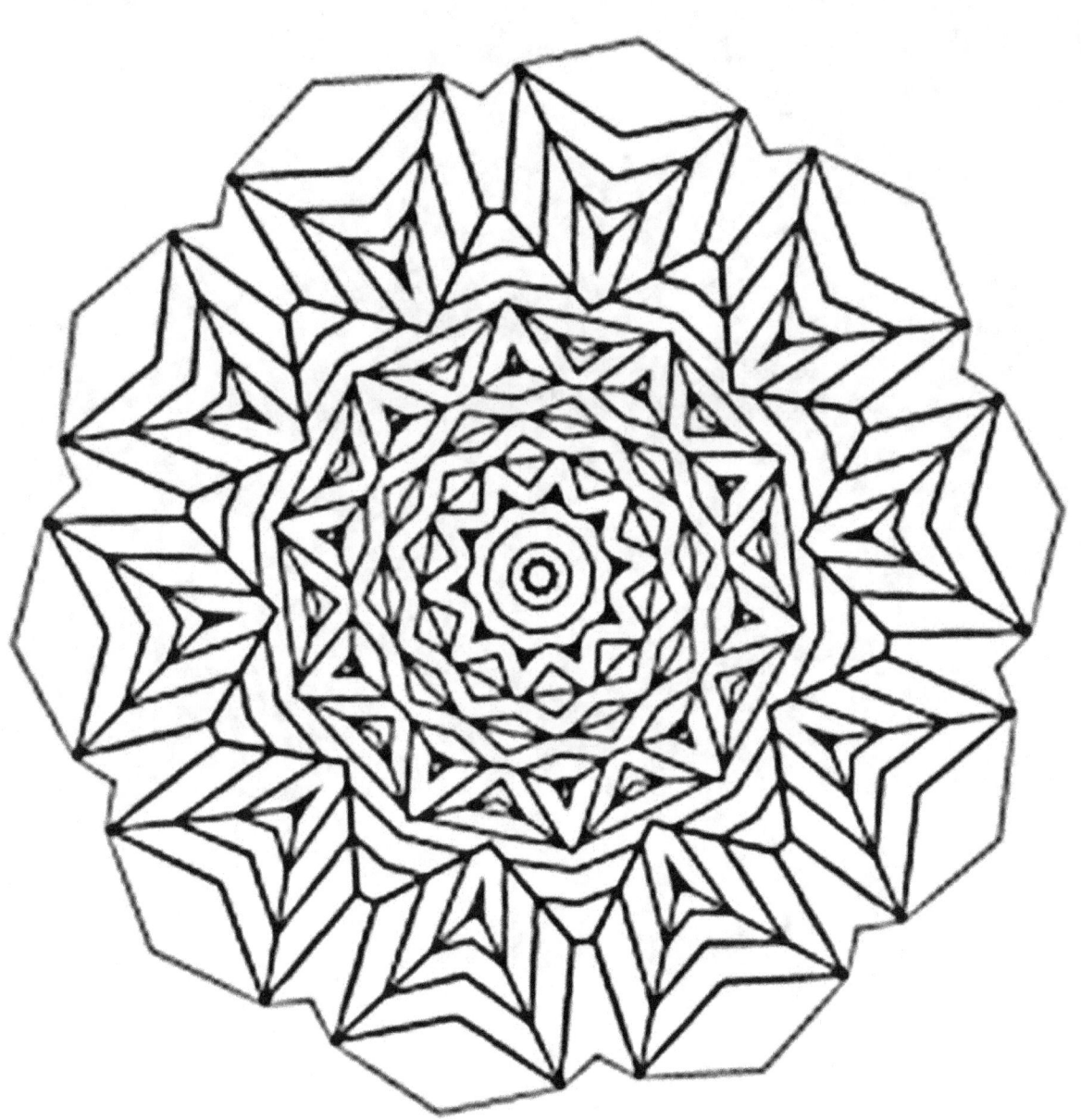

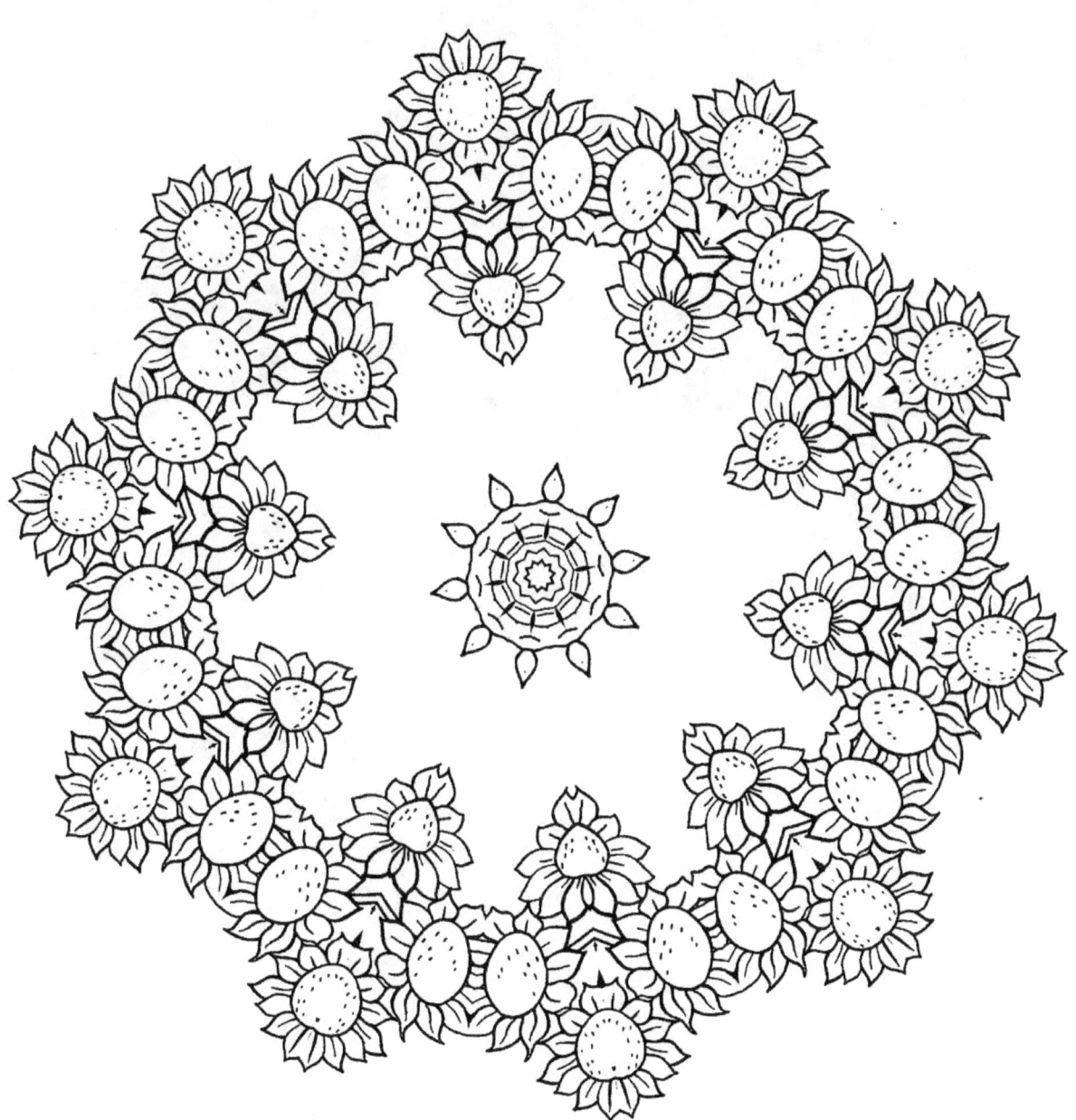

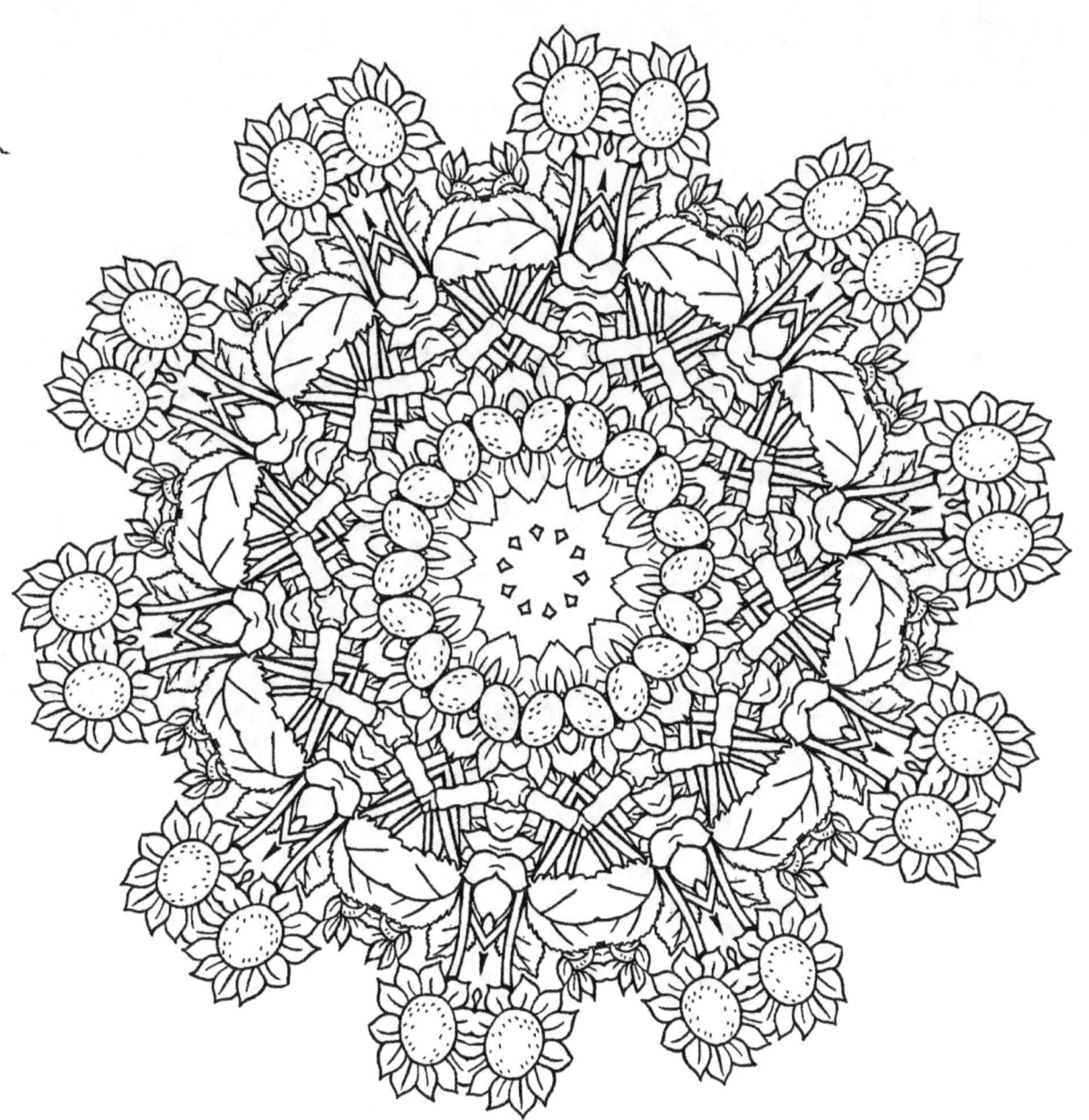

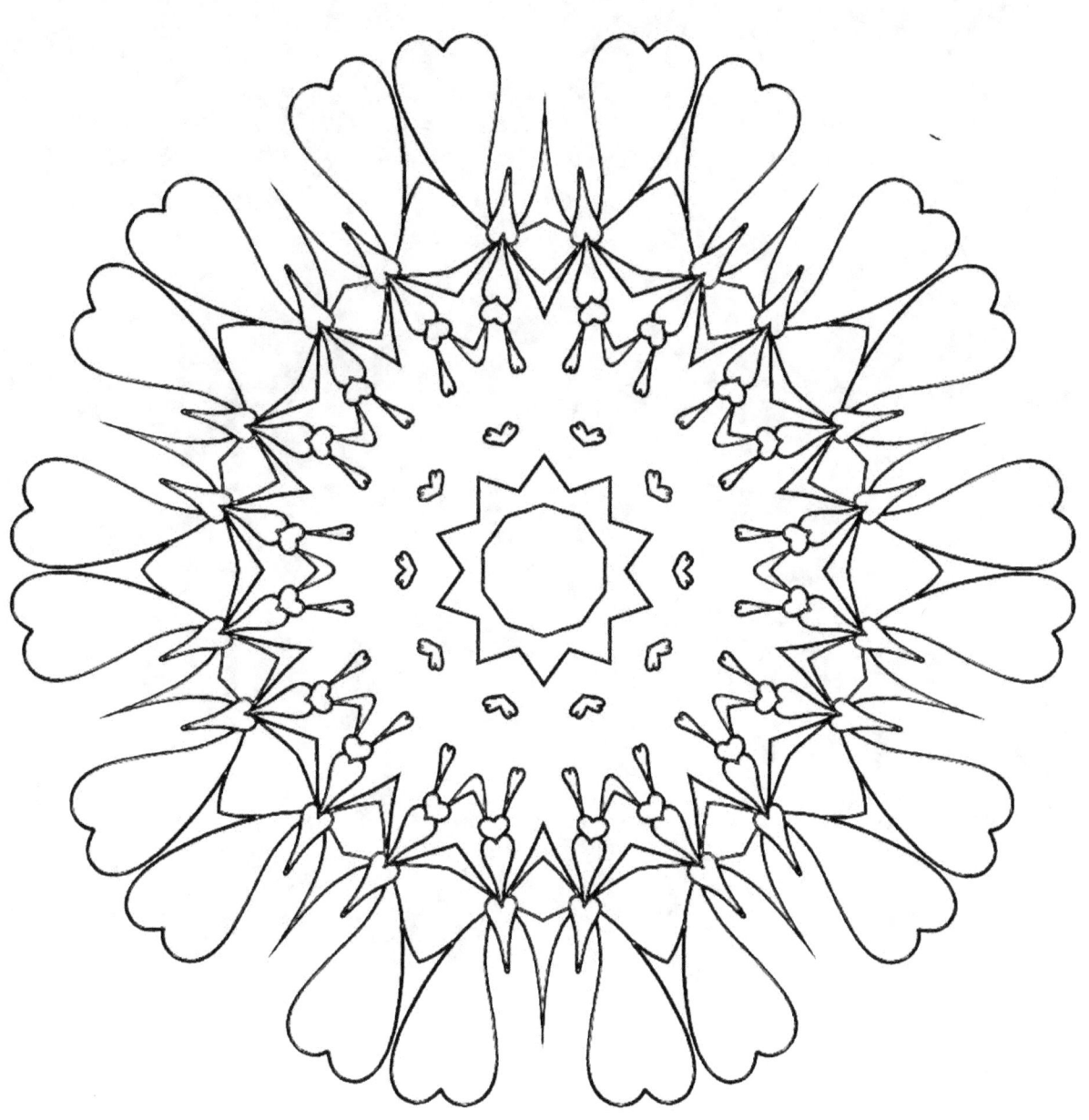

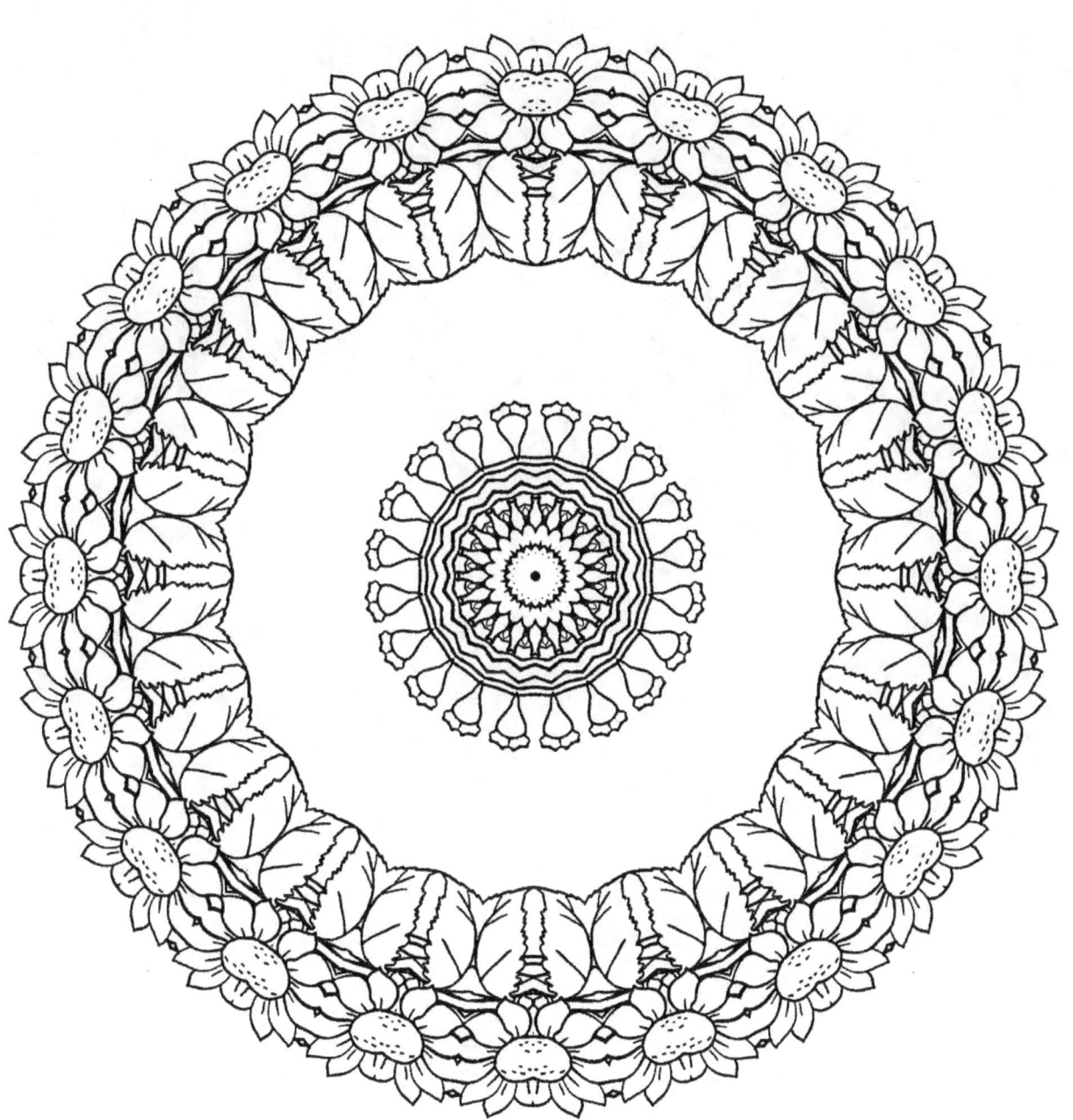

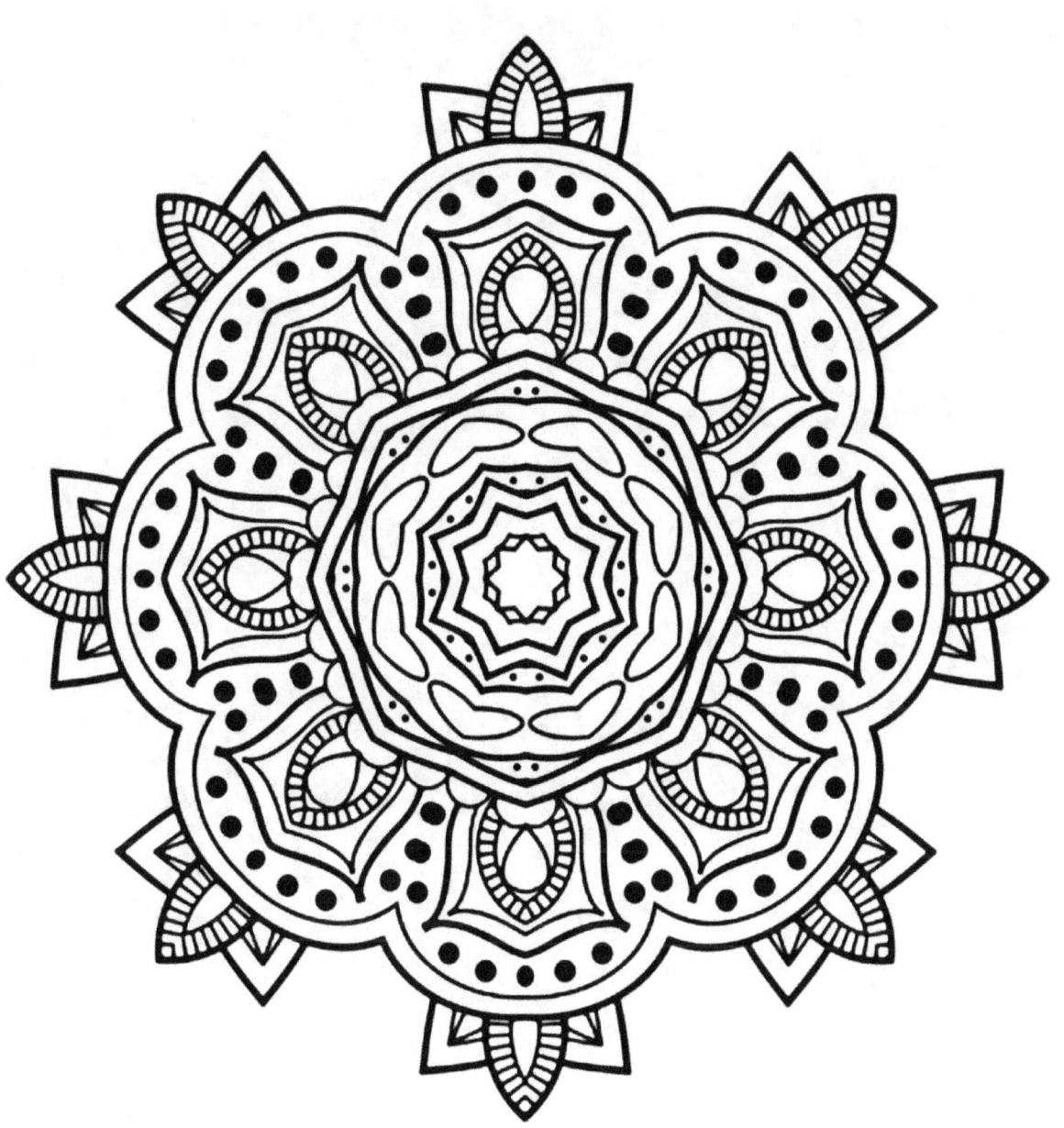

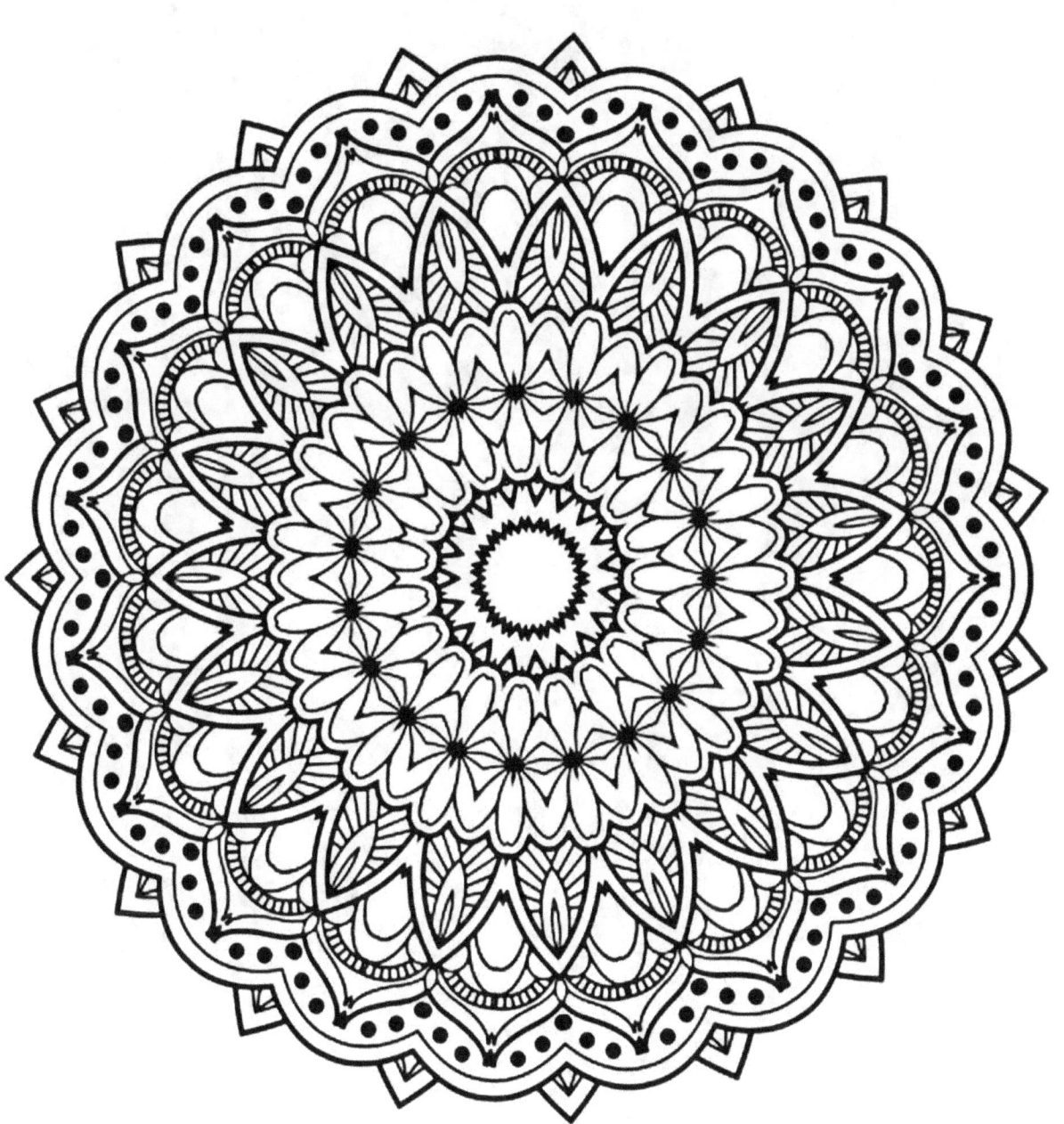

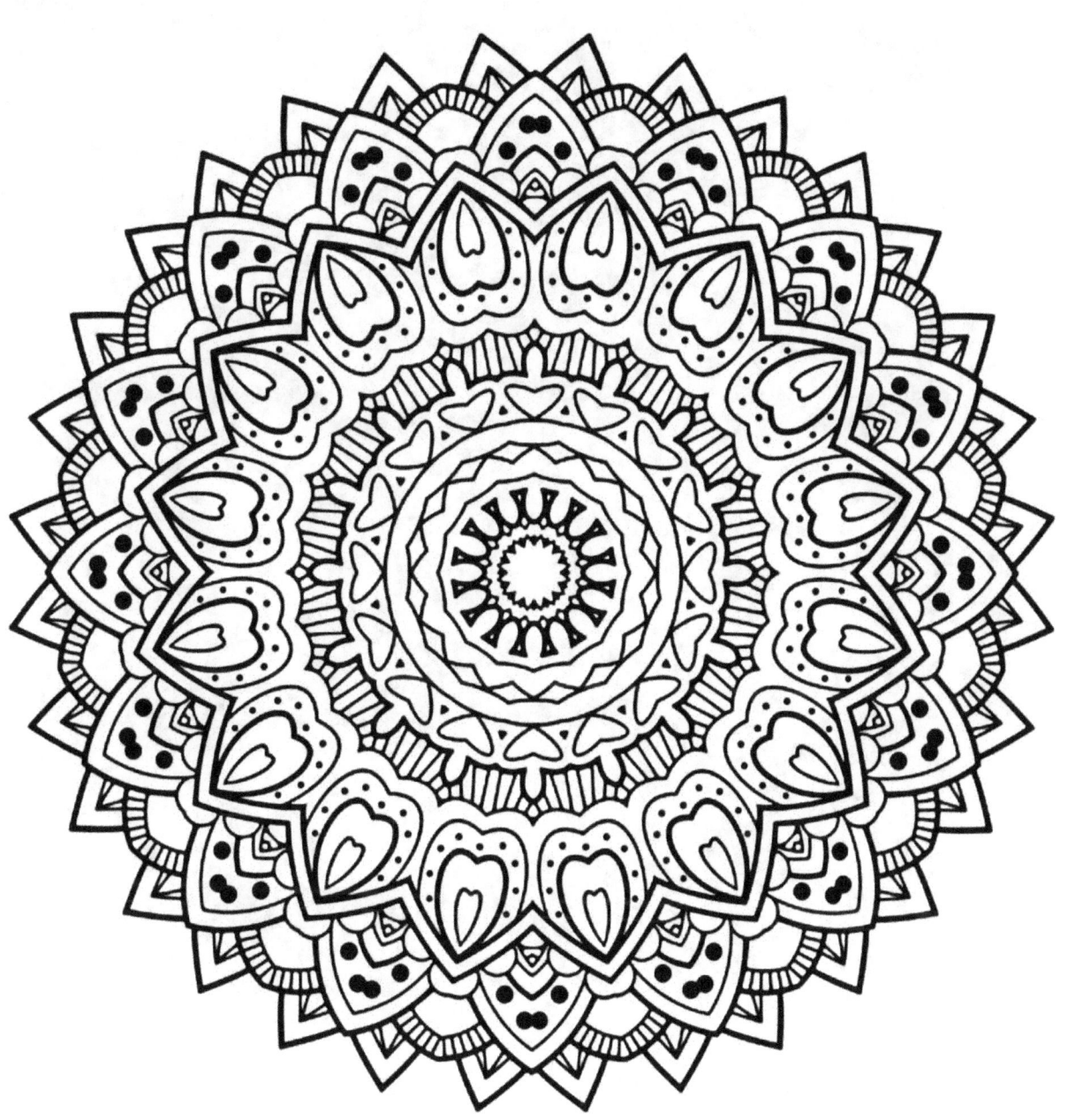

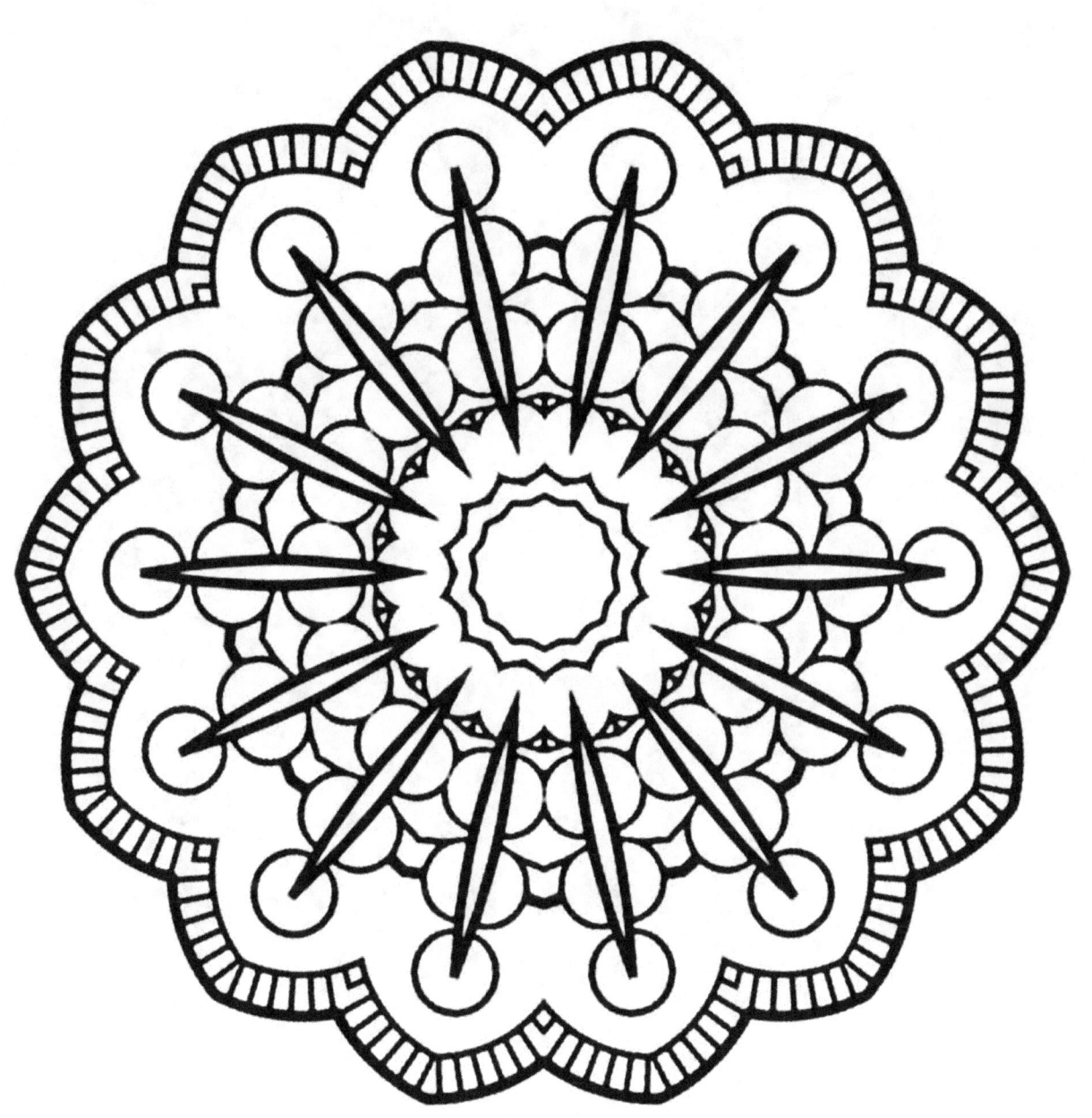

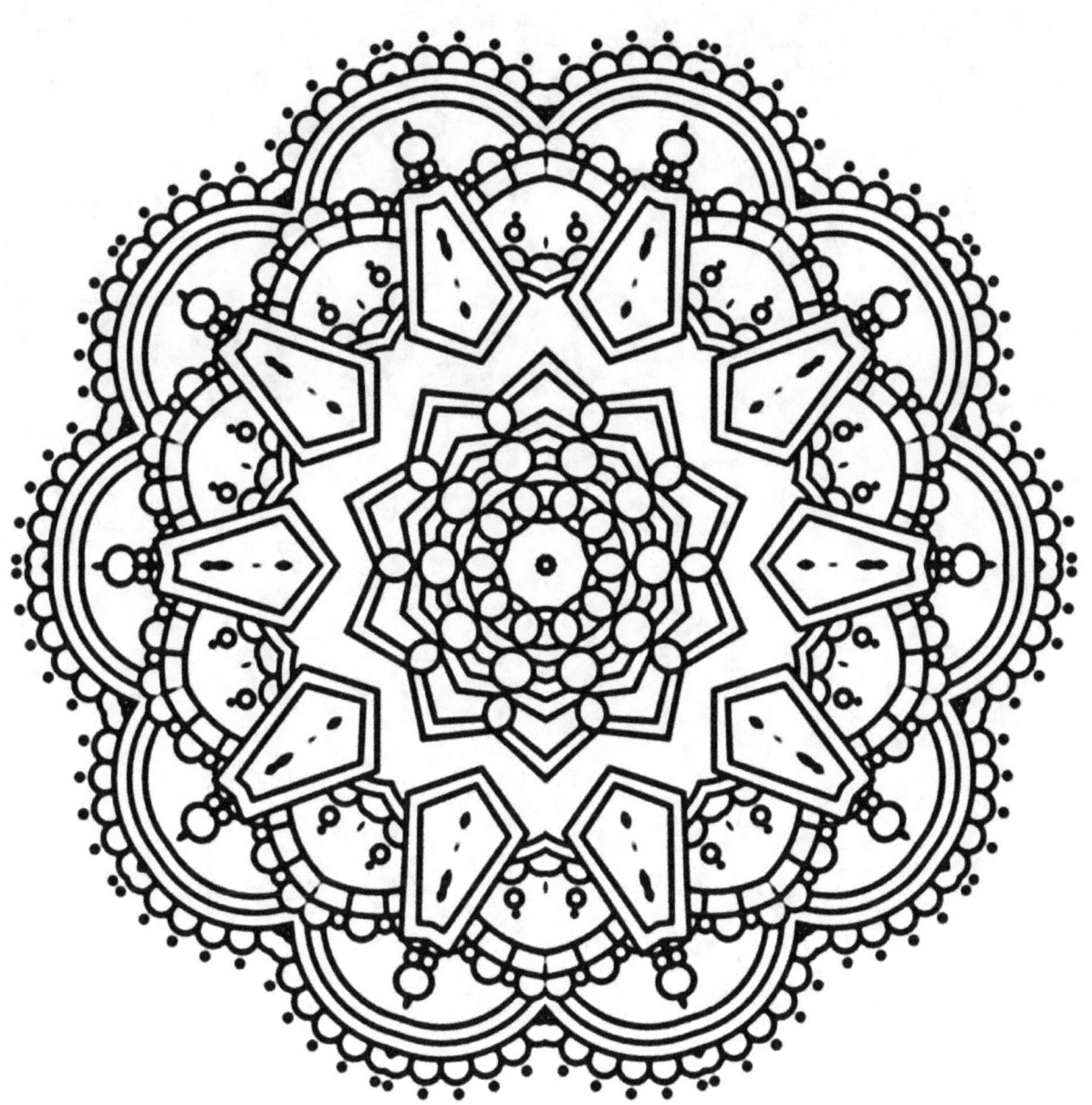

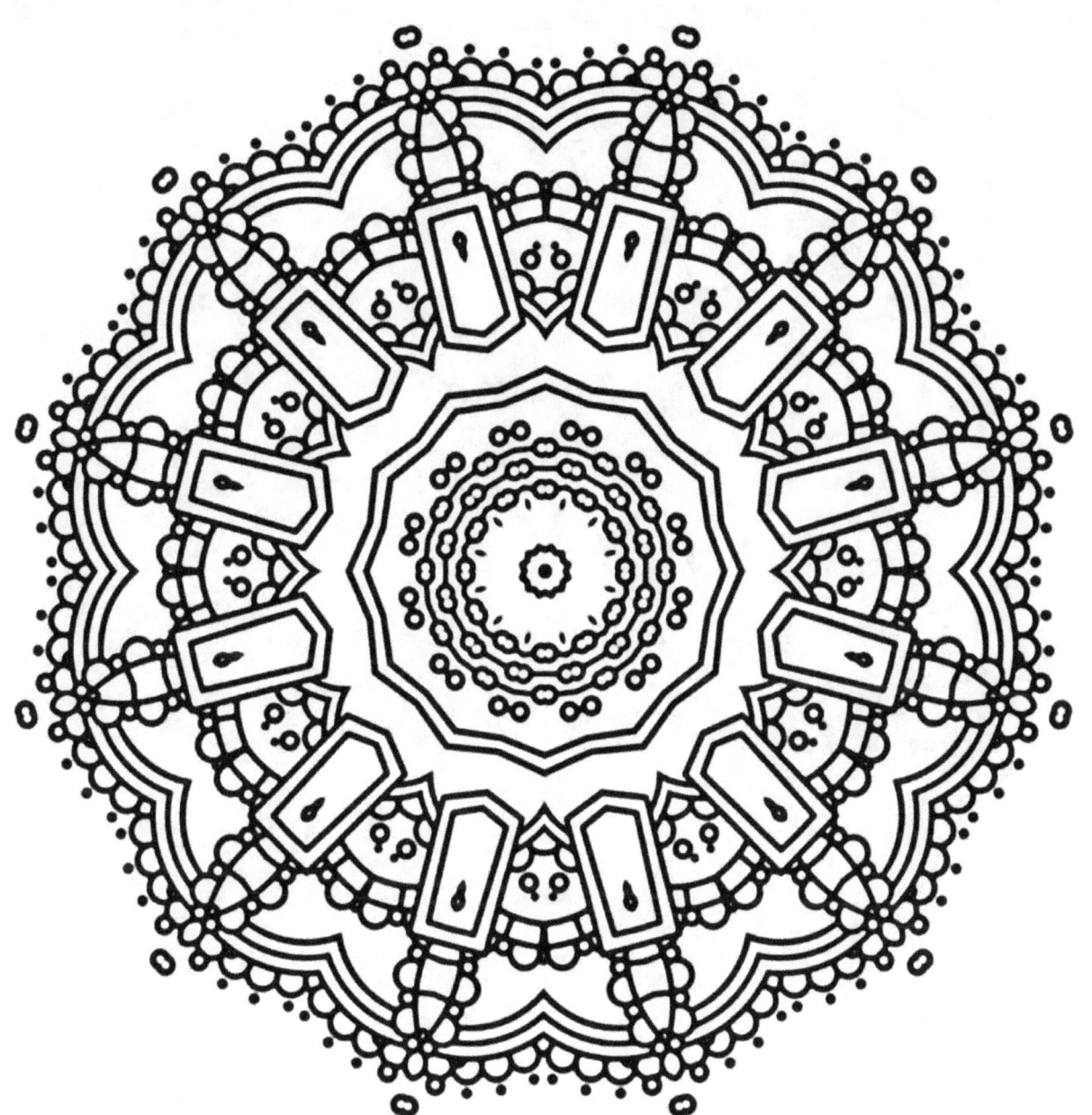

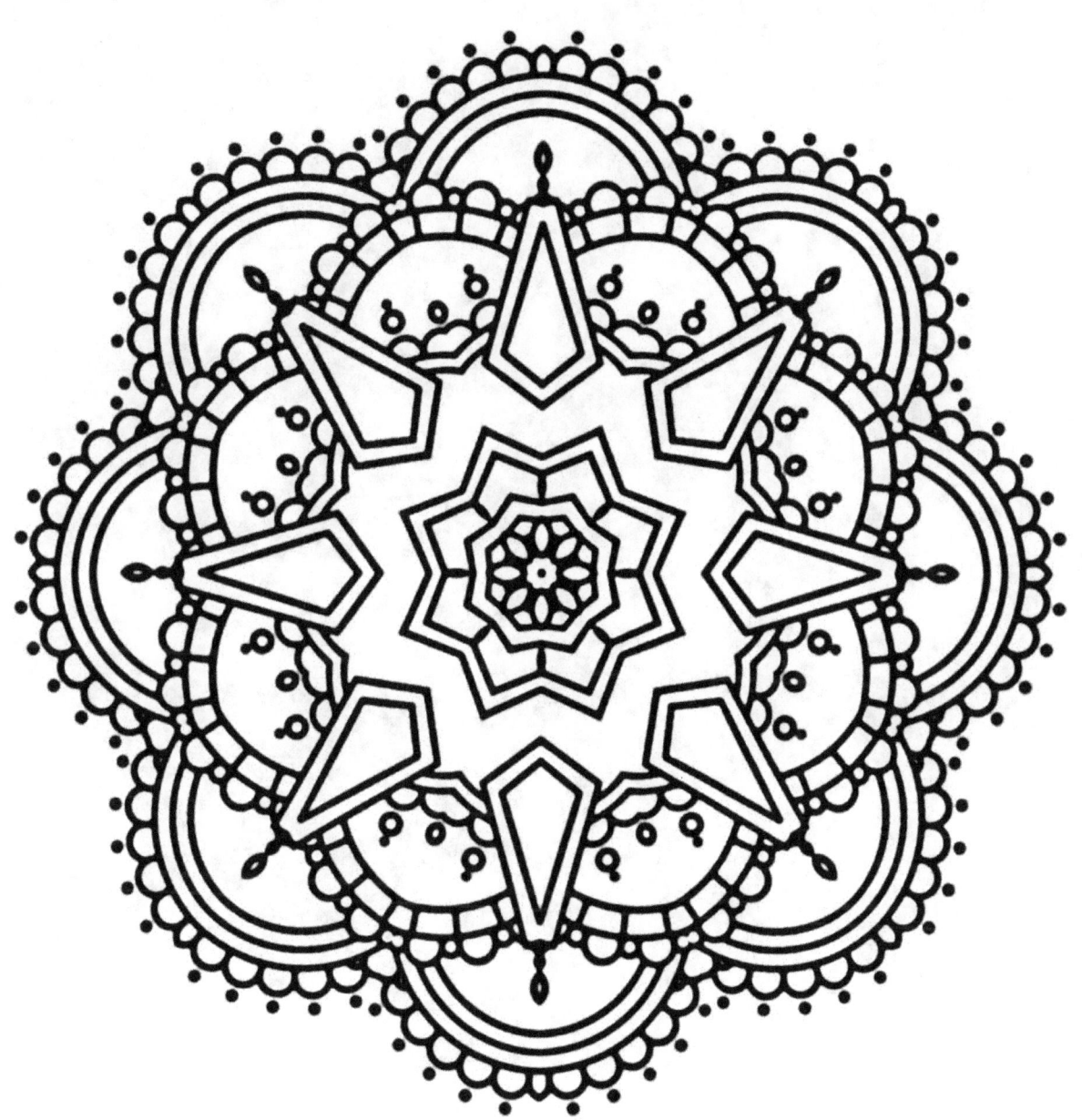

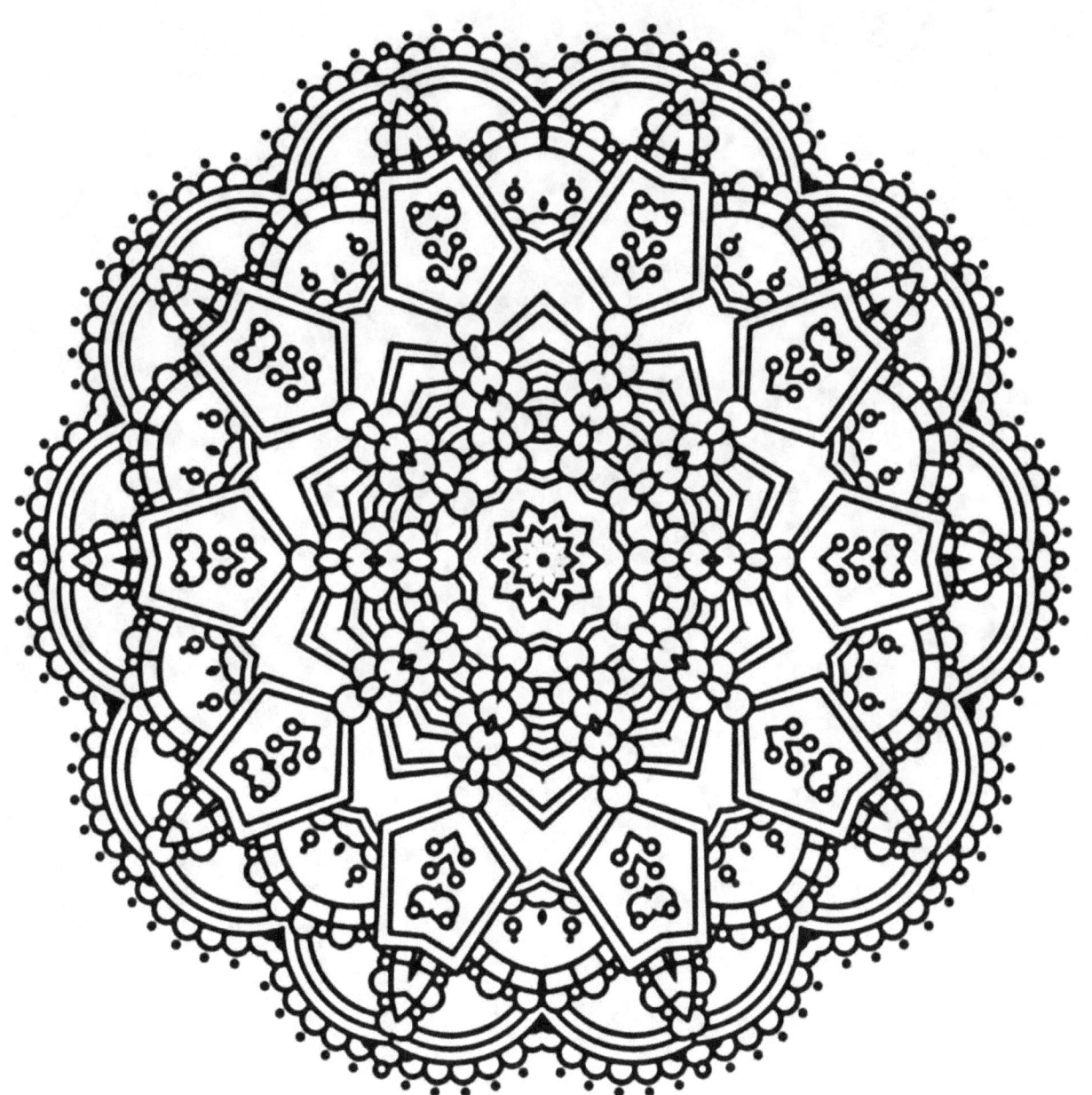

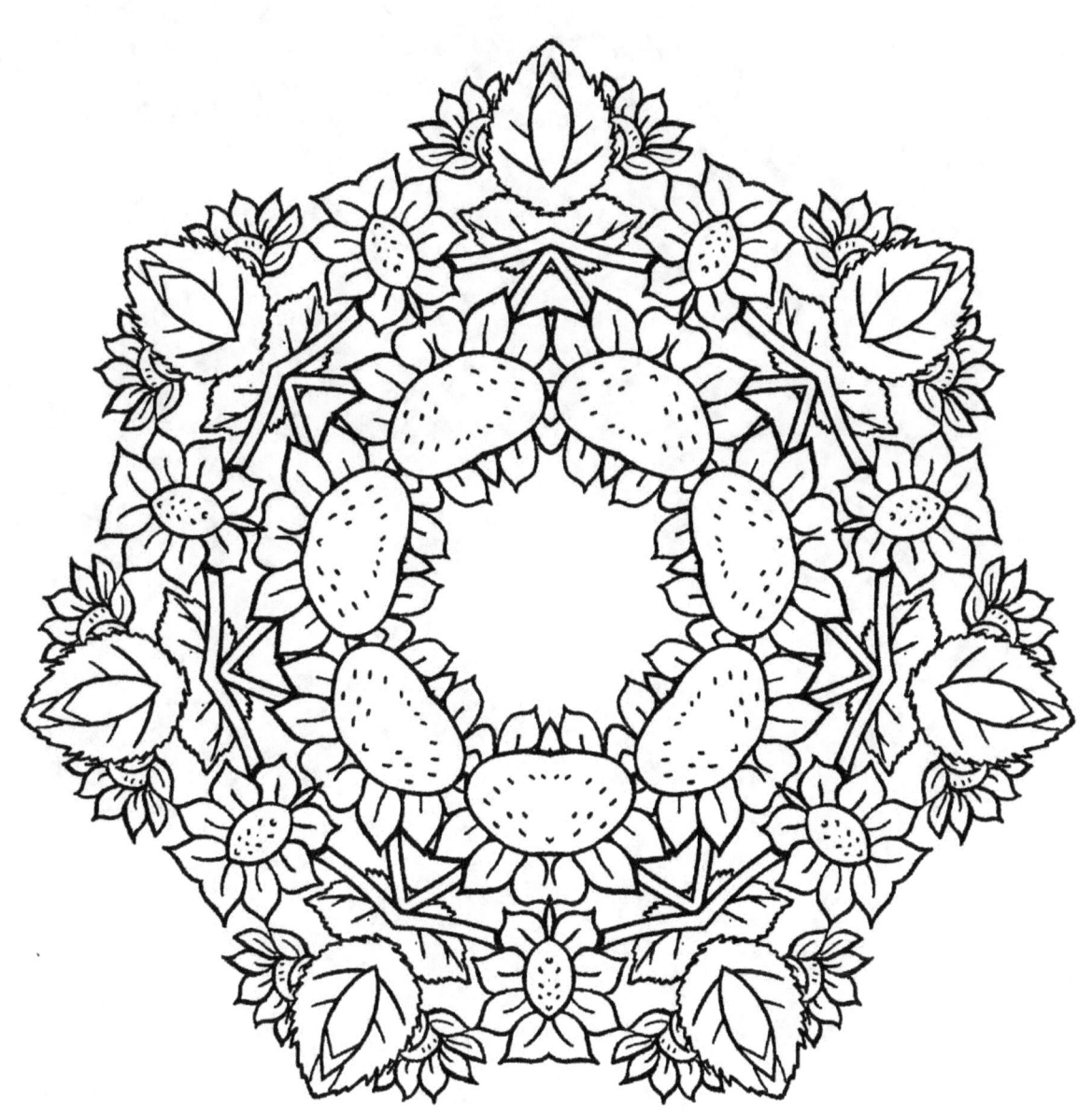

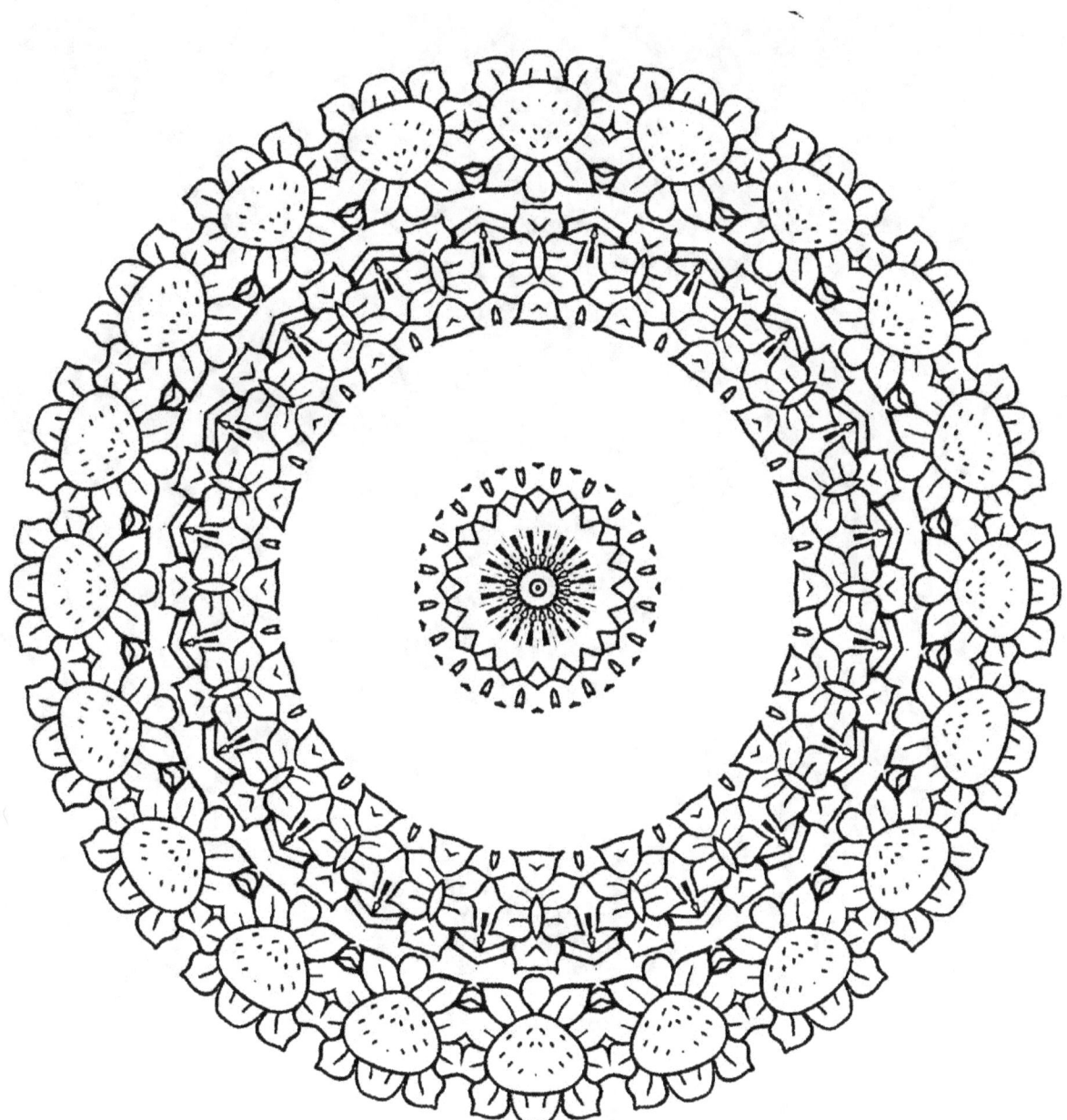

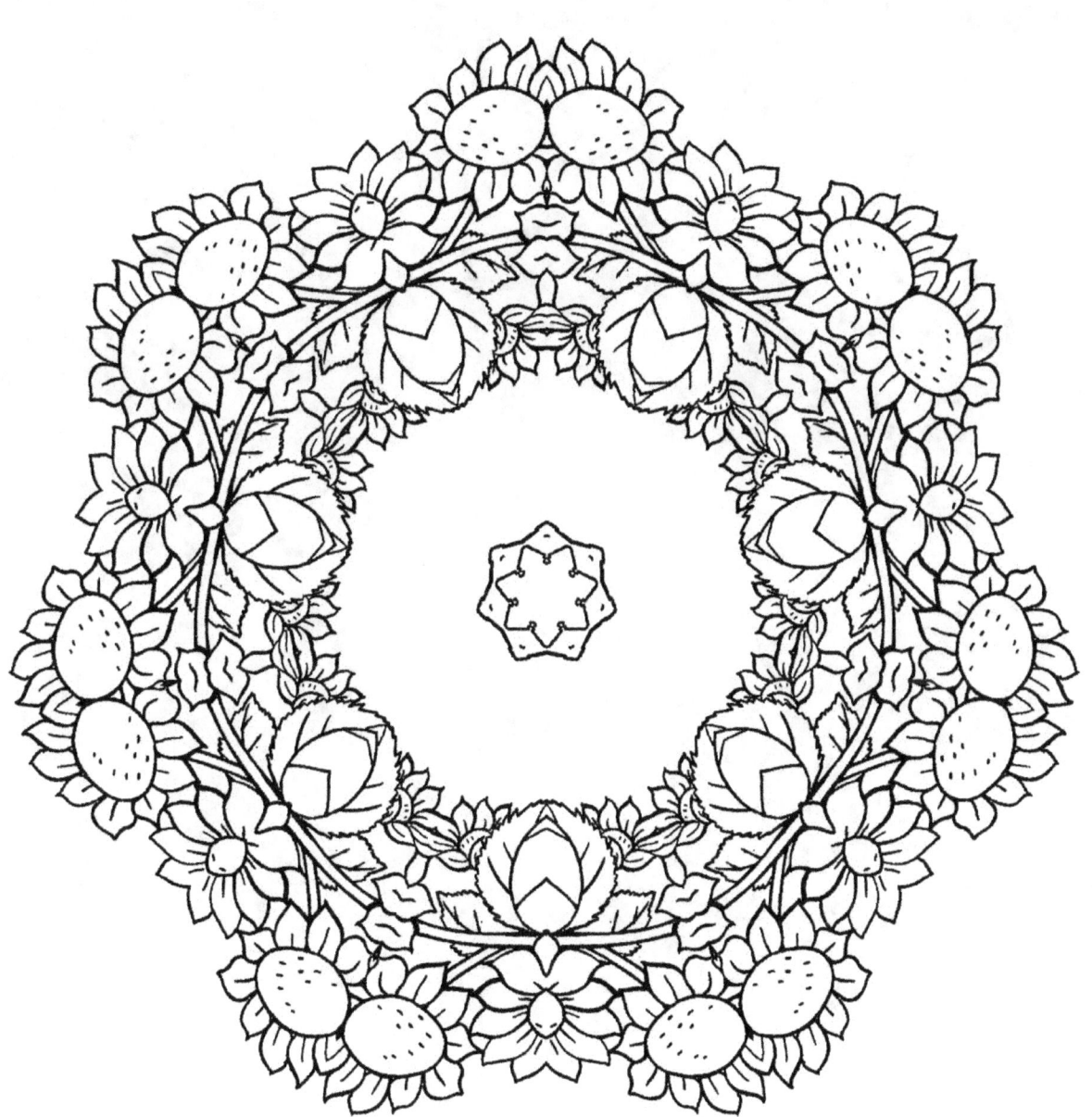

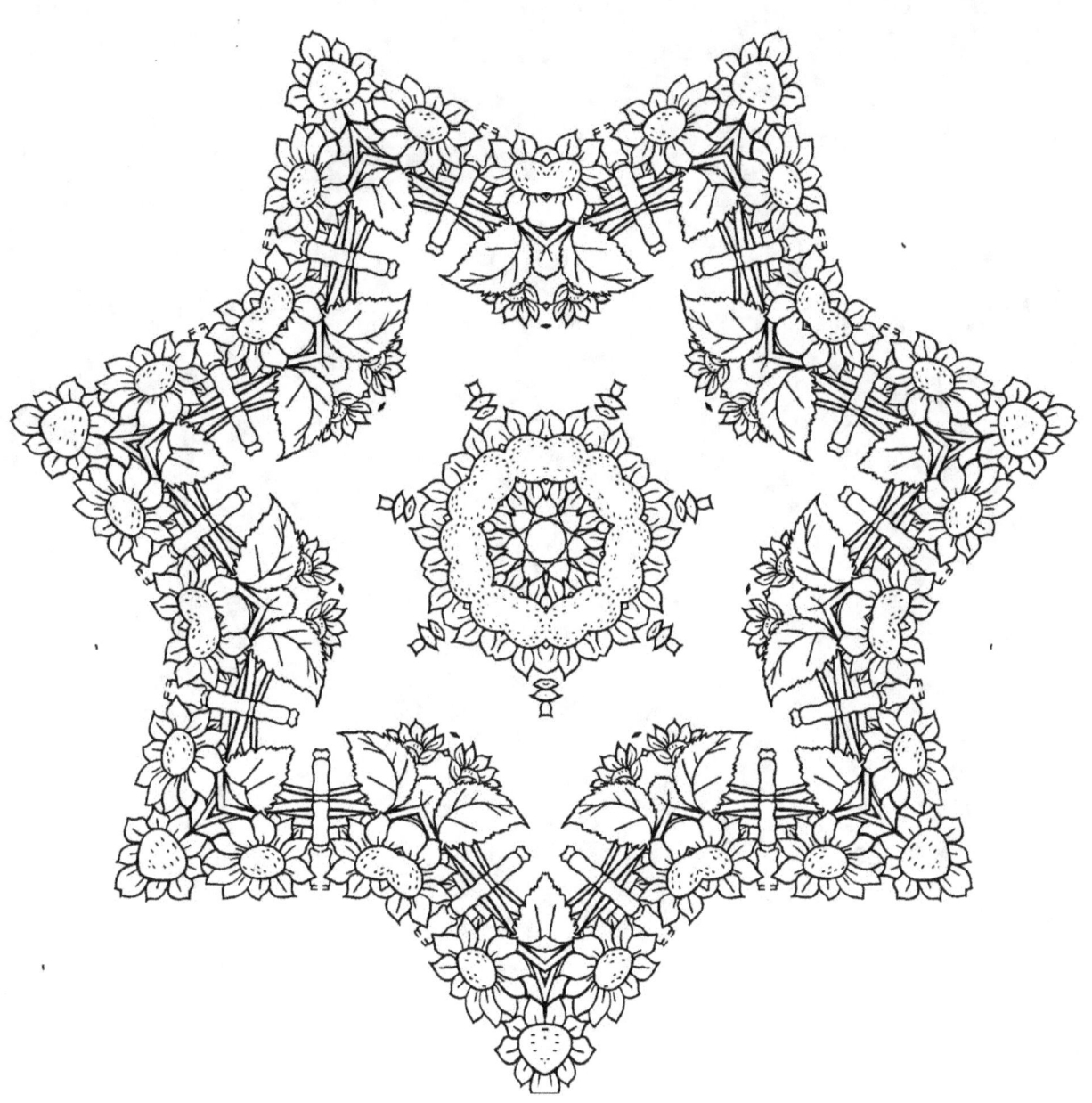

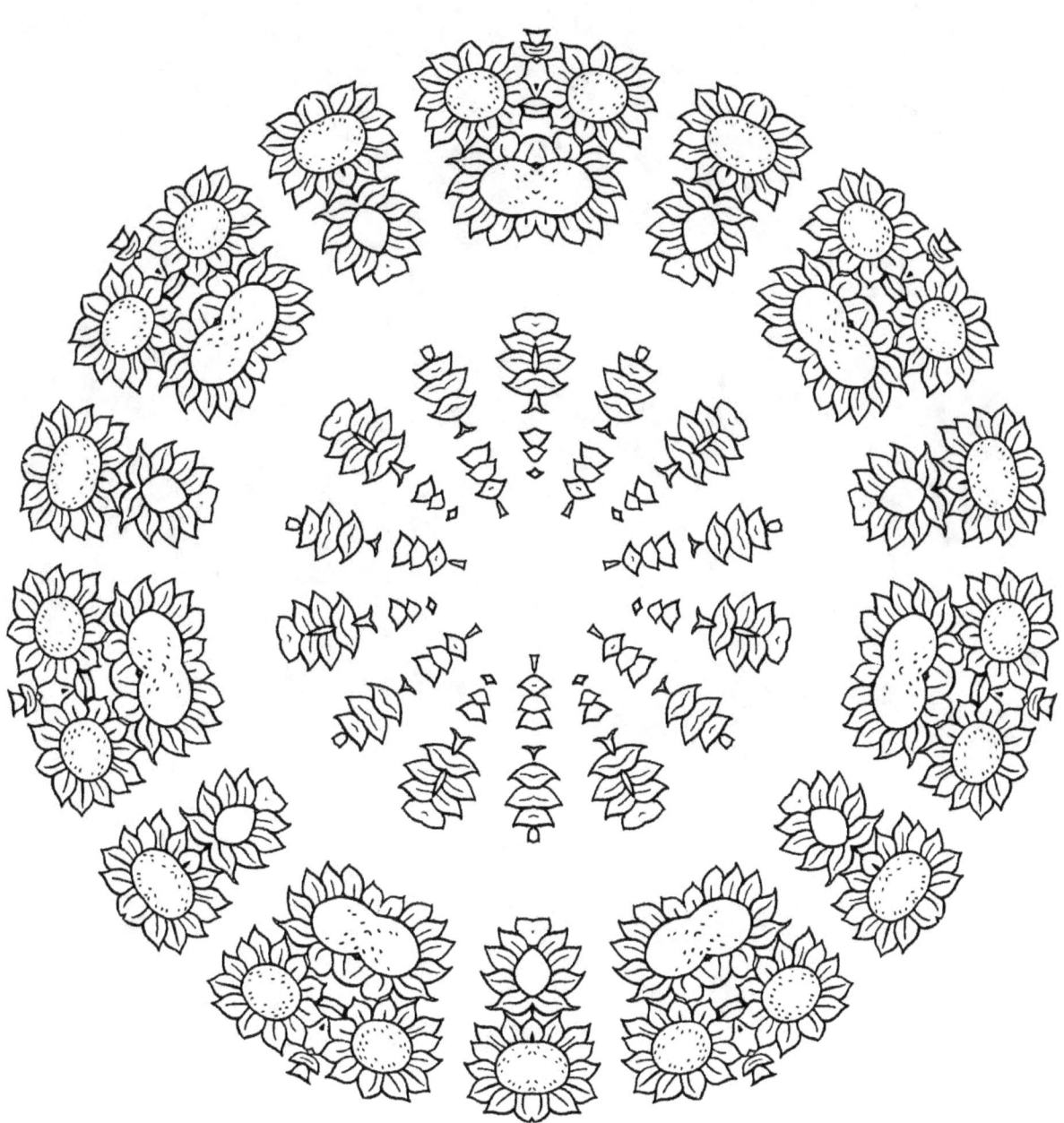

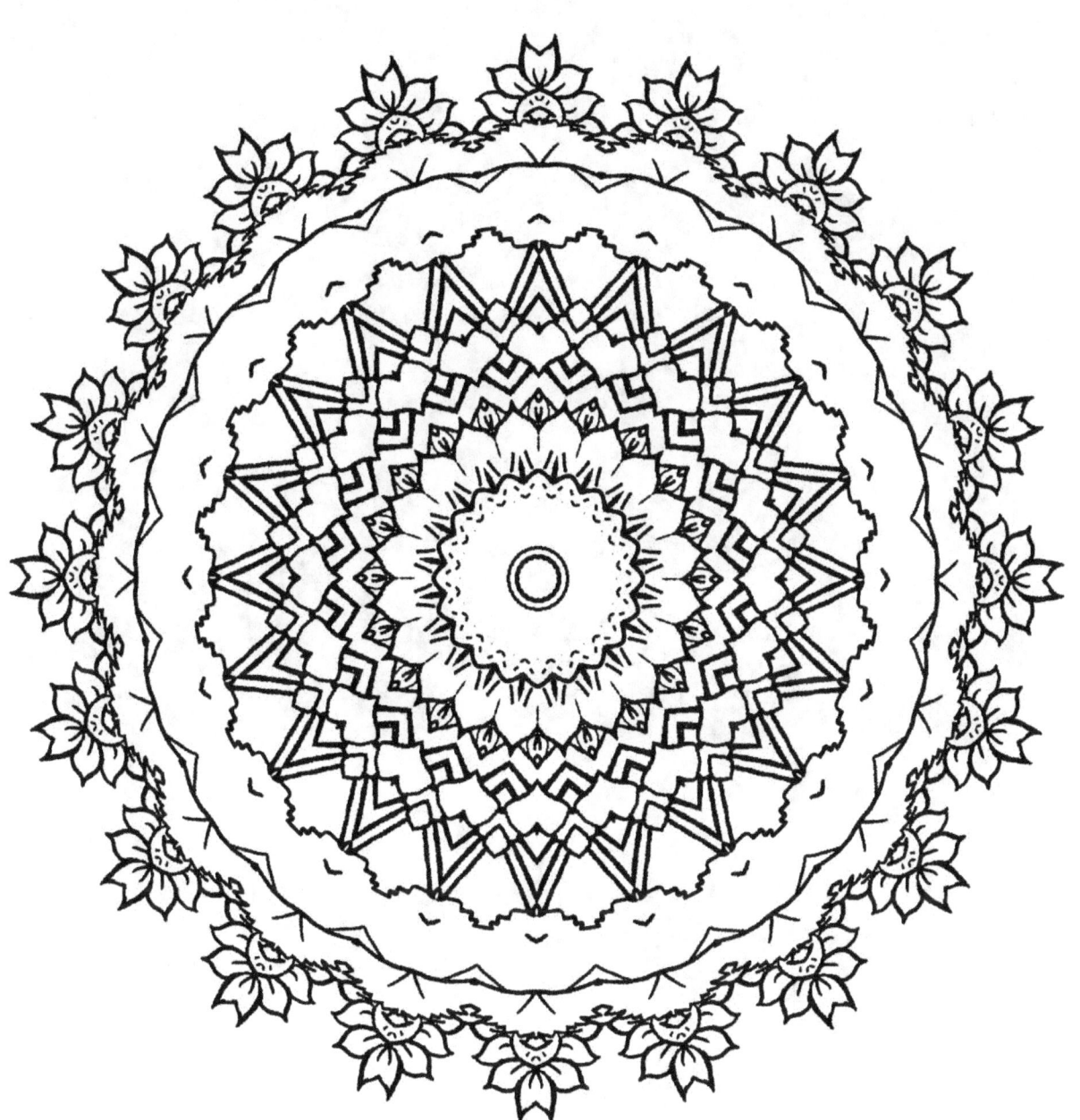

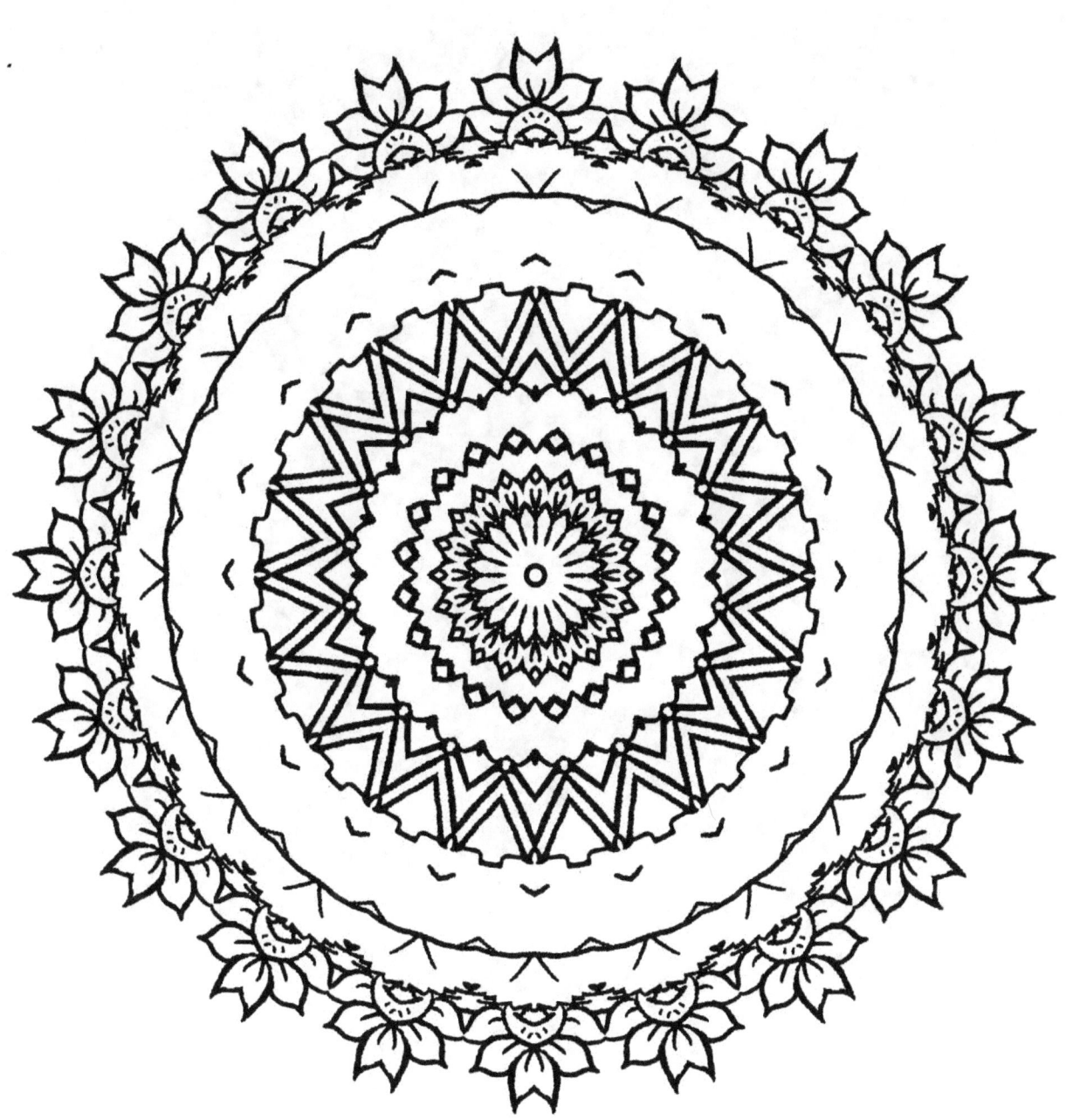

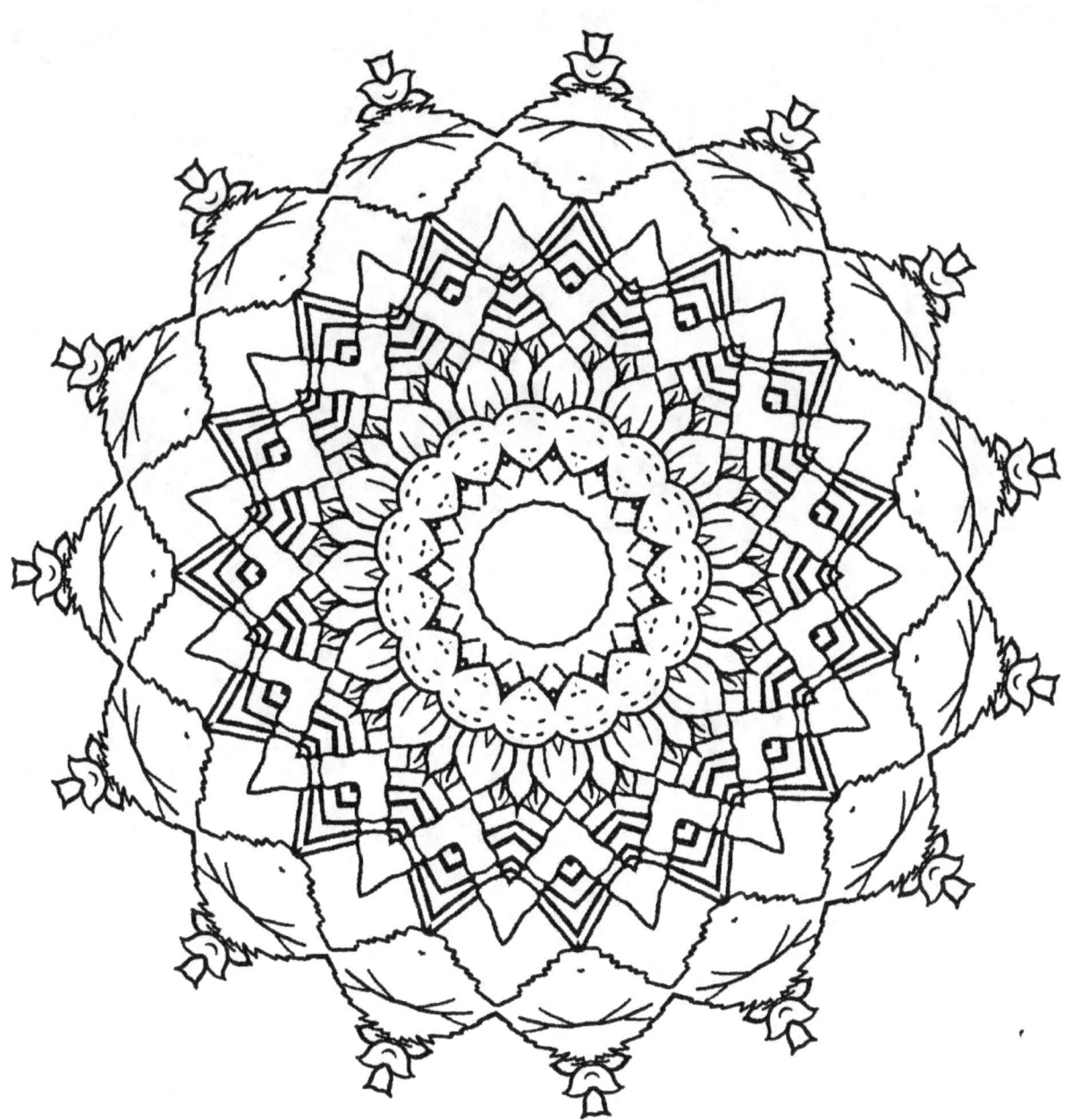

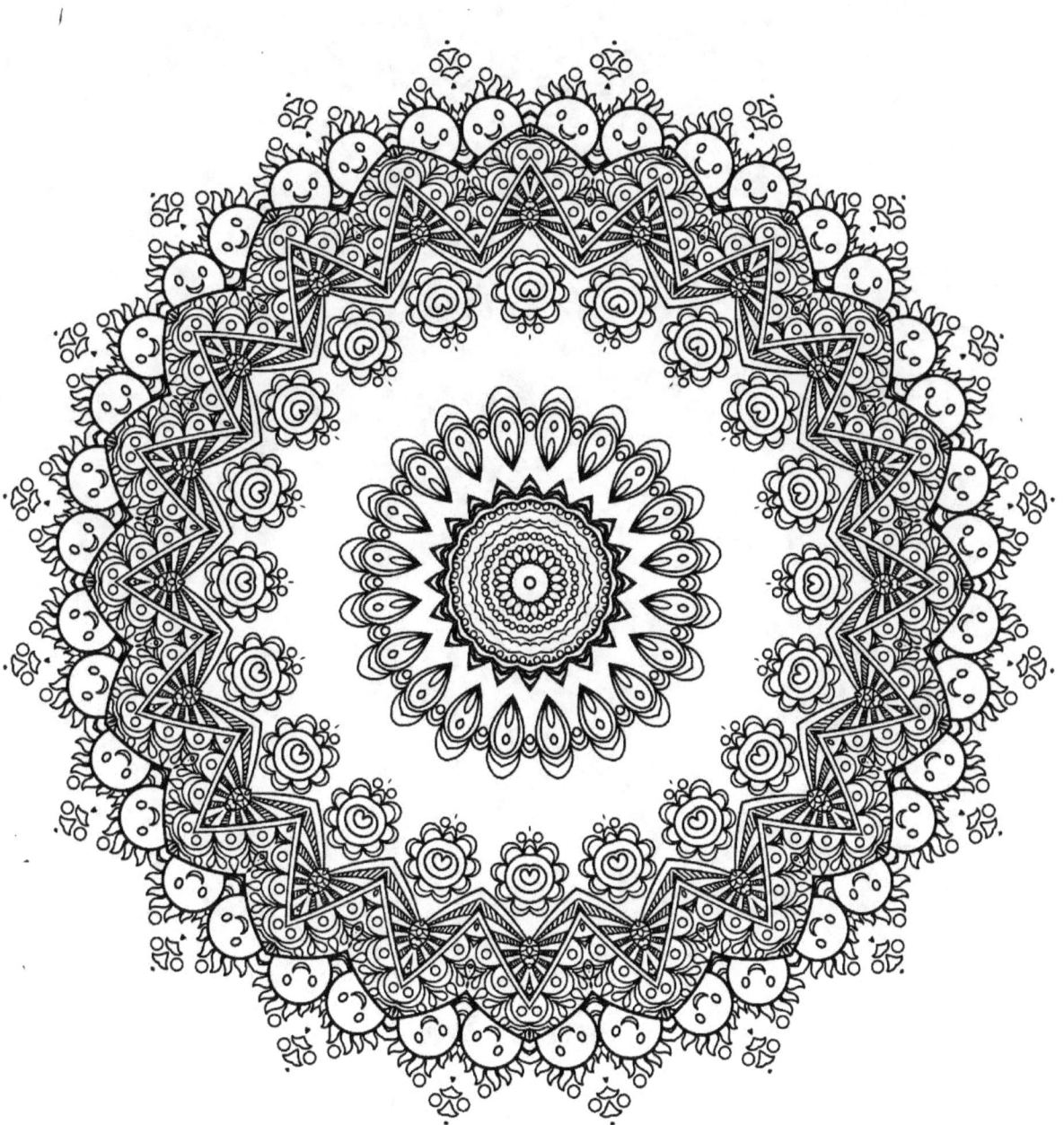

Thank you

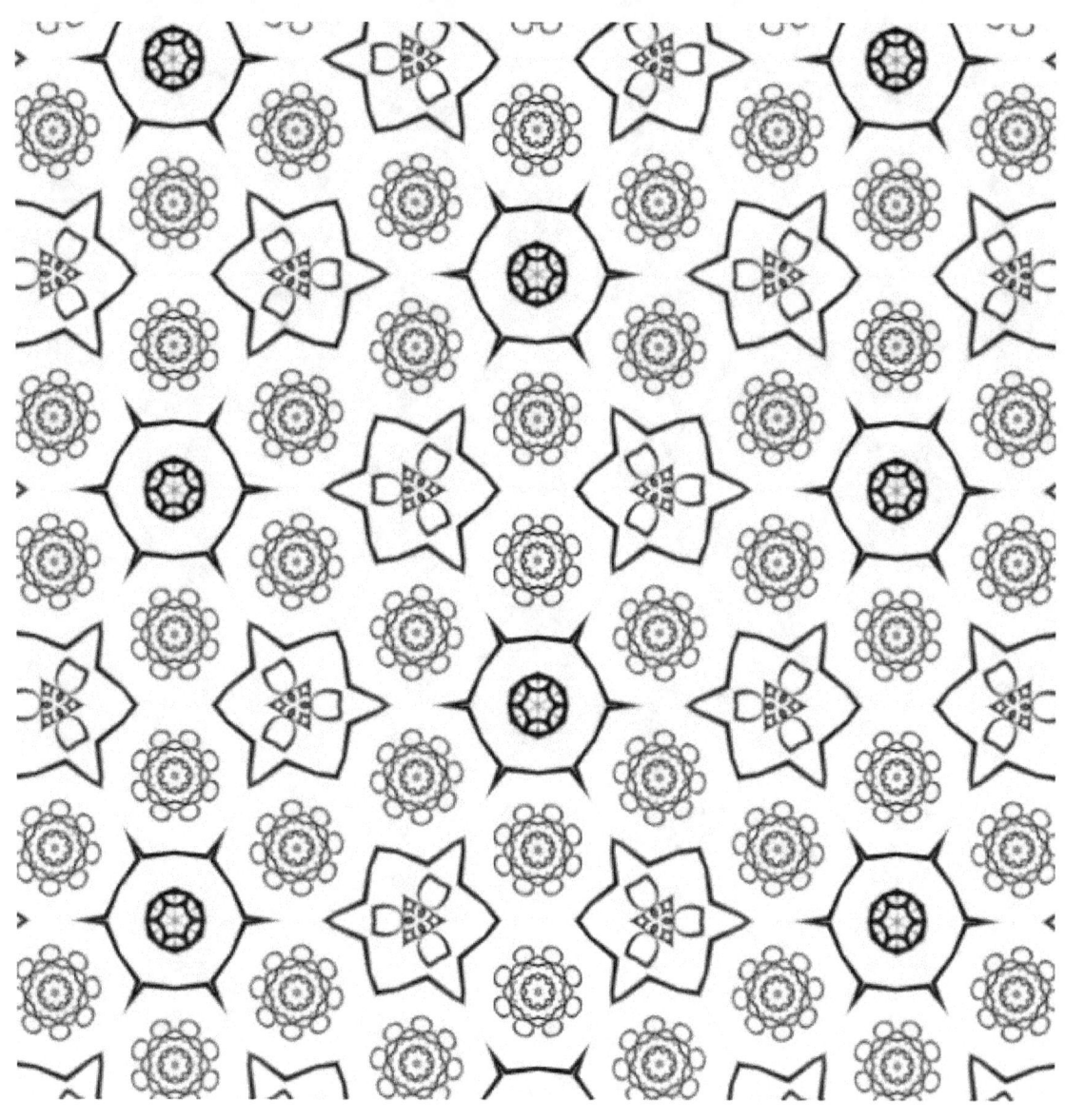